TRANSITION FOR PERSONS WITH DEAF BLINDNESS AND OTHER PROFOUND HANDICAPS: STATE OF THE ART

Papers from the National Conference on the Transition of Profoundly/Multiply Handicapped Deaf-Blind Youth, April 7-10, 1986, Pentagon City, VA

Edited By
Angela M. Covert
H. D. Bud Fredericks

Teaching Research Publications

Published and Distributed by
TEACHING RESEARCH PUBLICATIONS
345 North Monmouth Ave.
Monmouth, Oregon 97361

©Copyright 1987 by TEACHING RESEARCH PUBLICATIONS
ISBN: 0-944232-00-0
Library of Congress Card Catalog Number: 87-50630

Teaching Research pays careful attention to the information that we publish. It is our intention to produce material regarding all phases of special education in a manner that is easily understood and of the highest possible quality.

Library of Congress Cataloging-in-Publication Data.

Transitions for persons with deaf-blindness and other profound handicaps.

Papers presented at the proceedings of a conference held in Washington, D.C. in April 1986.

Includes bibliographies.
1. Blind-deaf--Services for--United States--Congresses.
2. Blind-deaf—Care—United States—Congresses. 3. Blind-deaf--Rehabilitation--United States--Congresses. 4. Blind-deaf—United States--Deinstitutionalization—Congresses.
I. Covert, Angela M.
II. Fredericks, H. D. Bud.
HV1597.T73   1987   362.4'18'0973   87-50630
ISBN 0-944232-00-0

Teaching Research is funded, in part, through a subcontract with T.A.S.H. (The Association for Persons with Severe Handicaps), Cooperative Agreement Number G0084C3001 by the U.S. Department of Education, OSERS, Special Education Programs.

The Helen Keller National Center's Technical Assistance Center is funded through Cooperative Agreement Number G0084C3002 by the U.S. Department of Education, OSERS, Special Education Programs. However, the opinions or policies expressed herein do not necessarily reflect those of the U.S. Department of Education.

CONTENTS

ACKNOWLEDGMENTS

This publication and the Conference that generated these papers would not have occurred without the support and leadership provided by program staff in the Office of Special Education Programs, U. S. Department of Education, and the Office of Maternal and Child Health Programs, U. S. Department of Health and Human Services. Specifically, we want to thank Dr. Merle McPherson, Dr. Thomas Behrens, Mr. Paul Thompson, and Mr. Charles Freeman. Each of these individuals devoted long hours to the planning and implementation of the Conference. All were active participants in the Conference, and their contributions were substantial. We are grateful to them.

We also wish to thank Terry Carr, Project Coordinator of the HKNC/TAC Project, for her enormous assistance in planning and organizing the Conference and in assembling all pieces for this publication. Her exceptional organizational skills and her attention to the overview as well as the detail kept us all on track.

Thanks also to Lori Doede, Publications Manager at Teaching Research, who helped make this publication a reality. With her fine editorial and management skills, she was able to take many pieces and make them into a cohesive whole.

And finally, we acknowledge the significant contributions of the presenters, the respondents, and the participants at the Conference. They gave of themselves and their time to address the difficult issues involved in providing quality transition services for young adults with deaf-blindness and other profound disabilities.

Angela M. Covert
H. D. Bud Fredericks

CONTRIBUTORS

Stephen S. Barrett, M.Ed., HKNC Technical Assistance Center, Sands Point, New York.

Hank A. Bersani Jr., Ph.D., Syracuse University, Syracuse, New York.

Joann Boughman, Ph.D., University of Maryland, Baltimore, Maryland.

Angela M. Covert, Ed.D., HKN Technical Assistance Center, Sands Point, New York.

Terrence R. Dolan, Ph.D., University of Wisconsin, Madison, Wisconsin.

Sharon Freagon, Ph.D., Northern Illinois University, DeKalb, Illinois.

H. D. Bud Fredericks, Ed.D., TASH Technical Assistance Central Office, Monmouth, Oregon.

Lori Goetz, Ph.D., San Francisco State University, San Francisco, California.

Janet W. Hill, Virginia Commonwealth University, Richmond, Virginia.

Sharon L. Hostler, M.D., Children's Rehabilitation Center, Charlottesville, Virginia.

Virginia Lapham, Ph.D., Georgetown University, Washington, D.C.

Kevin J. Lessard, Perkins School for the Blind, Watertown, Massachusetts.

Pamela Mathy-Laikko, University of Wisconsin, Madison, Wisconsin.

Nancy Norman, Iowa Commission for the Blind, Des Moines, Iowa.

Mary M. O'Donnell, New Jersey Association for the Deaf-Blind, Verona, New Jersey.

Lyle T. Romer, Ph.D., Neighborhood Living Project, Seattle, Washington.

Barbara Ryan, Special Education Resource Network, Riverside, California.

Rosanne Silberman, Ph.D., Hunter College--CUNY, New York, New York.

George H. S. Singer, Oregon Research Institute, Eugene, Oregon.

Paul Wehman, Ph.D., Virginia Commonwealth University, Richmond, Virginia.

INTRODUCTION

Angela M. Covert and H. D. Bud Fredericks

This book has as its genesis and basis the proceedings of a conference. The conference was held in Washington, D.C. during April 1986 and followed an invited, participatory format. In other words, all those invited were also participants in some capacity.

This book focuses upon the issues of transition for those with profound multiple-sensory impairments. The specific emphasis was on individuals known as deaf-blind and their specialized service needs. However, the issues and principles involved in programming for this population also apply to individuals with other kinds of profoundly handicapping conditions.

Transition has become the buzz word of the 1980s. It has been made a popular concept by Madeleine Will, whose office focused on the problems of vocational transition referring to the need for a "bridge" between the school and adult years. As a result, transition has become a principal discussion theme at major conferences; transition projects have been funded by the federal government; states have sponsored transition conferences and workshops; and professionals and parents alike have become sensitive to and concerned about the issues surrounding transition.

However, throughout this developing emphasis on transition, one population has been notably neglected—those who are the most severely impaired—those who are nonambulatory, and nonverbal and who possess few self-help or independent living skills and who in many instances are medically fragile. If one adds to this array of deficits the dual sensory impairments of vision and hearing, one uncovers a population for whom very few transition services have been planned or exist.

The lack of adult services for this population should not surprise us. In many schools, this population is still excluded. They are relegated to developmental centers or separate educational facilities. Moreover, there exists a body of educators who would maintain that they cannot benefit from education and should therefore not be in public schools. Thus, the exclusion from services afforded to others with severe handicaps is frequently the practiced solution for this population.

The deinstitutionalization movement has not altered their plight. If one tours institutions that have been significantly "downsized" one sees two populations remaining—those with severe behavior problems and those with profound and multiple handicaps.

There are few adult facilities or programs that provide services for those with profound handicaps. A number of reasons are offered: Sstaff are not trained to deal with them; there is an inadequate number of staff since this population needs one-to-one attention; the program is not designed for them. The latter reason is probably true in most cases. However, it would be more honest to state that frequently we do not know how to design the program for them. Few models exist that have demonstrated success, and little research data are available.

As a group of concerned professionals, we came together at this conference, mutually agreeing that individuals with deaf-blindness and other profound handicaps needed to be community based. We pooled our visions, our ideas, and our experiences and shared those with others in four major areas—residential, vocational, leisure and recreation, and health. We listened to presenters and reactors; we discussed and argued our various points of view; and we finally evolved concerns, issues, recommendations. This book contains these presentations, reactions, and the syntheses of the discussions of each of the four groups.

We share these with you, the reader, as a beginning point. We recognize that what remains to be done to provide an adequate array of services and a decent quality of life for this population is a monumental undertaking. However, in the past ten years we have made significant gains in providing for those with severe handicaps. We must continue to expand those gains and extend them to include those with profound handicaps.

KEYNOTE ADDRESS

Those with Profound Handicaps:
Who Are They? How Can They Be Served?

H. D. Bud Fredericks

The Purpose of This Conference

I believe that the lead speaker for this conference has the task of setting the tone of the conference, attempting to define the scope of the problem, indicating the difficulties of definition of the population, and suggesting what we are to try to succeed in doing during the next two days.

Our overall purpose is to define the issues regarding four areas: health, residential services, day employment, and recreation and leisure for those with profound handicaps and multisensory impairments. Those upon whom we are focusing are youth who are in transition; thus, we must consider programs that serve youth, and transitional services and the array of services for the adult population.

The Population under Discussion

Who are those with multisensory impairments and profound handicaps? The state of Georgia and the superintendent of public instruction of that fair state have determined that there are at least 150 of these people who cannot be educated in public schools and who should not receive such services. They have issued a directive that excludes them from public schools. We are talking about that population.

I should like to suggest that we may have some difficulty setting parameters around those with profound handicaps. Let me raise some issues regarding definitions of those with profound handicaps. My hope is that we might reach some consensus regarding this definitional problem.

Must those with profound and multiple sensory handicaps also be severely intellectually handicapped? Do we include those who are deaf and blind, but do not have an intellectual impairment?

The problem becomes more complex if we consider some other populations. Many of you have undoubtedly read about Annie McDonald in the book Annie's Coming Out by Rosemary Crossly. Annie was a child with severe cerebral palsy who lived in an institution in Australia. Annie's condition was such that given the non-care situation that she was in, her head was gradually turning back to her feet and she would eventually smother and kill herself. Rosemary Crossly was an aide in that institution who started communicating with Annie and other people and teaching them. They became known as the "bean bag" set. Rosemary Crossly demonstrated that Annie was intelligent. Does Annie represent a population that should be considered at this conference—a population so severely motorically involved that we frequently cannot discern their intelligence?

How about those who are severely autistically involved and who exhibit severe aggressive behaviors? In their own way, they are profoundly impaired in their communication abilities and their lack of appropriate social behavior. Yet, their motor skills are not impaired. Are they profoundly handicapped? Do we include those who are so profoundly behaviorally involved that they are excluded from most community-based programs?

How about the person who is severely handicapped but who is so self-injurious that most providers feel incapable of serving that person in the community? That person resides in an institution where successful programs for self-injurious behavior generally are not available. Should that person be included in the population under discussion?

And how about these students? Project them a couple of years to adulthood. Consider the seventeen-year-old in Oregon who is in a public school classroom, who is in a wheelchair, is nonverbal and who, every two hours, needs to be totally undressed and have rubbed over his body a lotion to assist the body temperature in maintaining some degree of normalcy. Consider the student in New York who is in the middle of the classroom with tubes connected to a machine located in the corner of the classroom. The student moves around the classroom and the other students avoid the long tubes leading to his body. How do we provide for these students when they become adults

4

in residential and vocational settings? How do we assist them to achieve meaningful recreational experiences?

There can be no doubt that the following describes a population whom we are addressing. This is taken from a Request for Proposals issued by one of the counties in Oregon for Adult Services: Persons to be served are nonambulatory, nonindependently mobile, needing to be fed, needing assistance in toileting, and needing daily physical, occupational or communication therapy.

Therefore, one of the problems which this conference faces is one of definition. Whom do we include? Whom do we not include and why?

Let us turn briefly to each of the strand areas--residential, health, vocational, and leisure. My purpose is to stimulate some consideration of each of these areas.

Residential

What type of housing is appropriate for those with profound handicaps and multiple sensory impairments? Small group home? Large group home? Is apartment living possible? How do we achieve the least restrictive living environment and how do we know that we have achieved it? How do we provide adequate health care on a continuing basis in a residential facility for the adult who is continually hooked up to some sort of tube? Is that person restricted to living in an intermediate care facility? I hope that we can be more innovative than that. The task of this conference is to suggest residential approaches that accommodate those with difficult health problems and profound handicaps.

What type of training is necessary for the staff of these residential facilities? Where do we obtain this training? Can federal initiatives help? What type of preservice training is needed? Who would provide it? How can we obtain sufficient inservice training?

Perhaps the easiest factor to address when one considers the residential option is the architectural one. We have been dealing with architectural barriers for such a long period of time that we have developed all types of innovative solutions. Not all have been implemented, but we generally know what needs to be done architecturally. The major problems in the residential strand relate to the nature of the program and the quality of the program. How do we ensure that we have that quality, and how do we measure it?

Vocational

Are sheltered work facilities the only option for those with profound handicaps? Have we any solid evidence which states that those with profound handicaps can succeed in a supported work environment? Can we provide community-based employment? Is employment the real issue, or is there some other type of day activity that is more appropriate for this population?

Certainly, some individuals with profound mental retardation have shown us that they can do some jobs in the community. Let me describe William. William did not relate to many people and in no case did he relate meaningfully, except to stare. When he was nineteen years old his teacher said, "William has no discrimination abilities at all. He can not discriminate up from down, back from front, black from white, round from square. He has not succeeded in any discrimination activity in the school." We placed William in a community vocational project at the Pepsi Cola Bottling Company. The task, associated with recycling, was to sort bottles that had been brought back to supermarkets and placed in bottle cases at random. These cases, which had been delivered to the bottling company, moved along a belt in front of the worker. The task of the worker was to remove the bottles from the case and put them by type and size into other cases. Most workers on the assembly line handled five or six different types of bottles. When William was first placed on the assembly line he was assigned the only bottle Pepsi Cola uses that has a unique color, the brown Jug Root Beer bottle.

William learned to discriminate that brown Jug Root Beer bottle within two days. Within 30 days he was discriminating five different types of soft drink bottles and was able to pick them out from the belt and put them in the appropriate box. William could work in the community, even though he was classified as being profoundly impaired.

But what of the person who is wheelchair bound, who has only one response with one hand and a very slow response at that? What is the hope for vocational placement? Who has demonstrated a successful vocational placement for this type of individual? How about the person whose only movement is with his/her eyes? How about the medically fragile person? How about the student in Oregon, the young man who must be disrobed every two hours and rubbed with lotion to help his body temperature? Is there any hope for vocational placement for him, or is his only appropriate facility a sheltered one? As I go from conference to conference and talk about adolescent vocational programs for those with severe handicaps, the same questions occur over and over. What about those with profound handicaps? What can we do for them in the community? What can we do that is not in a sheltered facility?

Leisure/Social

The issues here are difficult ones. If we accept the theory that self-injurious and/or assaultive behaviors are forms of communication, then perhaps the more community-based opportunities provided for youth with these problems, the more communication will be assisted. There are those who suggest they have evidence for that theory.

For the group who is nonambulatory and non-self-feeding, evidence exists for younger children that socialization can in fact occur. Dunst, Cushing, and Vance (1985) in Analysis and Intervention in Developmental Disabilities, demonstrated responses with six infants with profound handicaps using response contingencies. The effects on the parents were significant. The authors convincingly presented the implications for the need for extensive research and development in this area of communication. In JASH in 1983, Sternberg, Pegnatore, and Hill demonstrated the effectiveness of specific prelanguage communication programming techniques on the development of communication awareness behaviors in four students with profound handicaps. In the majority of cases, the communication awareness behaviors generalized to other situations and individuals. Thus, in the area of communication, which certainly is the forerunner of socialization, evidence exists that learning can occur to facilitate rudimentary socialization skills.

But the problems exceed communication. How do we provide access to the community for a tube-fed person? How can we teach others to communicate with those who have profound handicaps? How can we teach others to even want to communicate with those with profound handicaps? Many professionals today would advocate that those with severe and profound handicaps need to be socializing extensively with those who are not handicapped. I suggest that that type of socialization is very beneficial, but how do we achieve it? How do we do better than the "once a month for twenty minutes" session between someone who is profoundly handicapped and someone who is not handicapped and who also is not staff? How is that achieved? These I think are some of the issues that we must address in the recreation and leisure area.

Health

Health considerations pervade residential, vocational, and leisure time activities. How can we provide adequate health services across all of those activities? Eileen McDonald from the Yale University School of Medicine in 1985, in a survey of 27 persons with severe developmental disabilities residing in the community found a surprisingly low incidence of acute illnesses and emergencies. (I wonder if she would have found a different incidence among those with profound handicaps.) She pointed out that her data contradicted previous authors who had asserted that certain populations have excessive medical needs and therefore could not be served in the community. She concluded that community placement was advantageous to the group she studied since through placement they gained access to speciality medical services that had been previously unavailable to them as residents of a large public facility. Another question that needs to be raised about her study is whether those same medical services would be available in a rural setting.

Perhaps a more important question regarding health care concerns how we will pay for it all.

Common Issues

Some issues are common to all four strands. Let me suggest a few. How do we figure the cost of programs? How can we demonstrate cost effectiveness? Do we need to?

What about staffing; how do you use paraprofessionals? I am always very pleased with Oregon's Rural Aide Model. That model was developed to provide classroom services in public schools in rural areas in Oregon for those with moderate to profound handicaps. The data that have been gathered from that program indicate that students served by an aide in a rural setting without a certified special education teacher have progressed as well as those who are served by special education teachers in more populous areas. The Rural Aide Model is one that some cities have adopted to allow students to go to their neighborhood schools. The rural aide concept may be applicable to those with profound handicaps in not only rural, but also urban, areas. We must consider the delivery of adequate services across all types of geographic areas.

Related services need to be considered. How are they to be delivered on a continuing basis? Who is to deliver them? What type of a model do we recommend for the delivery of those services? What type of model produces the best results? Do we really know the answer to the latter question?

Finally, how do we convince existing providers that they need to serve those with profound handicaps? We may have a major attitudinal obstacle to overcome. Suggestions regarding how to change those attitudes are desperately needed.

In this conference we have a formidible task ahead of us. During the next two days, I hope we may provide the beginning of a significant impact on the entire field. I hope that, as a result of this conference, we will have been able to define the issues and be able to stimulate better service for those with profound handicaps and those who are deaf and blind.

I would like to close by reading briefly from one of my favorite authors, Ann Turnbull:

Kevin . . . an adolescent . . . is severely retarded, receives kidney dialysis five times per day and is tube fed six times per day. He is homebound and requires diligent supervision to insure that he does not pull his tubes out, bang his head or pull his hair. For the last several months our family has been providing respite care for him on a periodic basis . . . . Kevin unwittingly peeled off all of our defenses . . . the protections that we thought we had developed by reason of being adults, parents, and professionals. We had no power, no authority, no credentials to fall back upon. In essence, Kevin was in control of us, not we of him. All that he had left us was our common denominator with him, which is our humanity. It is all we had, just our humanity in the presence of his own. Confronting ourselves that way was threatening. It was not a question of whether we would take care of him, or whether we could keep him from injuring himself. Nor was it a question of whether we could have a more desirable effect, comforting him and bringing joy to him. No, the questions were more direct. Would we be able to relate to him as one human to another? Would we see him to be like us in the most fundamental way? Was his profound disability an acceptable way for him to be—was Kevin an acceptable human being?

We had help in answering these questions from Kate, our seven year-old-daughter . . . . Listen to Kate's diary:

I went to Kevin's house on July 30th. I went with my Mom and Dad. I went to help take care of him and to play with him. Kevin is fifteen years old, and he is a very nice sweet boy. He's very gentle, but it scares me sometimes when he hurts himself like pulling his hair and banging his head on some wood (bed frames). His kidneys don't work so he's on dialysis and he doesn't like to eat much so there is a tube that goes down in his nose and the food goes down in there. The funnest part was taking him for a walk in his stroller. I just noticed something on the first night, that he liked to pull things apart. I gave him some flowers and he kept pulling stems and petals off and it really was interesting . . . . There are a lot of people who don't want to go to Kevin's house because they think they can't handle him, but he's just a very sweet and nice and gentle person. He is also so happy and bright that it makes me enjoy life more and you know it makes me be happy and bright also when I go over to his house . . . . The first time I saw him I was scared because of all the tubes that went into his head and went into his nose. But now I'm not scared at all.

Perhaps one of our major tasks at this conference is to convince the rest of the world to be as accepting as Kate. If so, we might be able to make a major difference in the lives of those with profound handicaps.

References

Dunst, C., Cushing, P., & Vance, S. (1985). Response-contingent learning in profoundly handicapped infants: A social systems perspective. Analysis and Intervention in Developmental Disabilities, 5, 33-47.

McDonald, E. (1985). Medical needs of severely developmentally disabled persons residing in the community. American Journal of Mental Deficiency, 90, 171-176.

Sternberg, L., Pegnatore, L., & Hill, C. (1983). Establishing interactive communication behaviors with profoundly mentally handicapped students. The Journal of the Association for the Severely Handicapped, 8, 39-46.

Turnbull, A., & Turnbull, H. (1985). Stepping back from early intervention: An ethical perspective. Keynote paper presented at the DEC/CEC Early Childhood Conference, Denver.

SECTION I. COMMUNITY-BASED RESIDENTIAL OPTIONS

Community-based Residential Options
for Persons with Severe/Multiple Disabilities:
Impact of Services on Peoples' Lifestyles

Lyle T. Romer

Introduction

Over the past 10 years residential services for people with disabilities have undergone a notable shift in direction. Approximately 6,000 persons per year have moved from large, publicly operated residential facilities to programs providing residential services in community settings (Hill, Lakin, & Bruininks, 1984). These authors also report that residential programs are becoming smaller, with a mean of 25 residents in 1978 and 18 in 1982. These changes in size reflect decreases in the numbers of people living in public facilities serving 16 or more residents, only minimal growth in private facilities serving 16 or more residents and, most notably, an increase in the number of people served in privately operated programs for less than 16 residents. Despite these changes in location of services and size of programs, 64.5% of those receiving services still reside in facilities serving 16 or more persons, with 58.4% living in programs serving 64 or more residents (Hauber, Bruininks, Hill, Lakin, Scheerenberger, & White, 1984). If these trends toward smaller numbers and movement to community settings continue, then community programs will be offering services to increasing numbers of people with severe and profound disabilities, since these people constitute the majority of those still residing in the large public and private facilities serving 16 or more individuals (Hauber et al., 1984).

The principle of normalization (Bank-Mikkelson, 1969; Nirje, 1969; Wolfensberger, 1972) has provided the major philosophical orientation for the deinstitutionalization movement in this country. Normalization states that citizens with handicaps should have access to the same rights and benefits that are available to all other members of society. In addition to equal rights, normalization supports the use of ". . . means which are as culturally normative as possible, in order to establish, enable, or support behaviors, appearances and interpretations which are as culturally normative as possible . . ." (Wolfensberger, 1980, p. 80). Deinstitutionalization became a direct outgrowth of normalization in that it was not considered normative to live in ". . . a place of residence and work where a large number of like-situated individuals, cut off from the wider society for an appreciable period of time, together lead an enclosed, formally administered round of life . . ." (Goffman, 1961, p. xiii).

The deinstitutionalization movement has addressed itself to the means for achieving normalization but has nothing to tell us about the influence of this movement upon the quality of life experienced by the persons who have moved. Research programs designed to investigate the success of deinstitutionalization will have little to offer to the future development of residential support programs unless the features of a successful program are identified. Success can be specified in terms of the features of a residential program, changes in the characteristics of the people who receive services from programs, or the ways in which service recipients lead their lives. We have to accept the responsibility of specifying what outcomes we expect from our residential programs before we are capable of determining the most effective means for achieving these intended outcomes. In order to specify where we want to go, we must be able to identify what is valued for people with disabilities. Certainly, no one has the right to specify what is valued in another person's life in any specific sense, but we should be willing and able to identify the framework we will employ for individuals and/or their advocates to make these determinations. Several frameworks for specifying the features of successful programs have been developed and employed. The next section of this paper critically examines these frameworks.

The development of this paper was supported in part by Grant G008430096 awarded to the University of Oregon, Specialized Training Program from the Office of Special Education and Rehabilitative Services, U.S. Department of Education. However, the opinions expressed herein do not necessarily reflect the position or policy of the Department and no official endorsement should be inferred.

Evaluating Residential Programs

Bellamy, Newton, and Lebaron (1985) have proposed a structure for examining the various ways to evaluate the impact of residential programs on the lives of their service recipients. They describe three categories of measures of quality in program evaluation: capacity, progress, and lifestyle. While there may be some degree of overlap among these, they are useful for both examining the current state of program evaluation and also for designing a comprehensive evaluation plan.

Capacity as a Measure of Quality

Evaluation based on capacity looks at a program's physical attributes and procedures that are assumed to bring about normalized outcomes for people served. Items such as the size and location of a home are assessed, as well as the presence of appropriate procedures for resident admissions, safety plans, number and classifications of staff, and so on. If one were to assess physical integration through a capacity measurement approach, one would evaluate whether the home were located in or near population centers and near community resources. ACMRDD, CARF, and ICF/MR regulations are probably the most widely used measures of a program's capacity for providing quality services. Several other capacity measures have appeared in the recent literature: the Multidimensional Environmental Assessment Procedure (Moos & Lemke, 1979), PASS 3 (Wolfensberger & Glenn, 1975), PASSING (Wolfensberger & Thomas, 1983), Resident Management Practices Scale (King, Raynes, & Tiard, 1971), Index of the Physical Environment (Pratt, Luszcz, & Brown, 1980), and MacEachron's (1983) physical environment index adapted from Morris (1969) and Gunzburg and Gunzburg (1973). All of these capacity measures enjoy one and the same advantage: They are easily administered. They also provide some information that may not be assessed in ongoing measures of quality and resident lifestyles, such as the comfort and attractiveness of the home, staff practices toward residents, and the presence of adequate safety features to minimize the likelihood of atrocities occurring. The major disadvantage of relying solely on capacity measures for evaluation is that they never directly measure the resident's quality of life. It is quite possible to have a program located in the heart of a suburban neighborhood, but, in actuality, residents may only leave the grounds of the home each morning by a special transportation system to be taken to a segregated school or sheltered workshop, to return home in the late afternoon by the same transportation system. Staff, instead of residents, may do all of the functions that would normally require physical integration such as grocery shopping, banking, dealing with social service agencies, and so on. Some programs, most notably ICF/MRs, may even provide services in the home that are usually acquired in the community, such as medical examinations by the program's consulting physician, haircuts, and exercise activities in the home's therapy pool instead of at the pool at the YMCA. Lastly, the capacity measures will not necessarily ensure the same level of opportunity for people with severe and profound disabilities as they might for people with milder disabilities. While it may be sufficient for people with mild disabilities to be close enough to community services to be able to use them, residents with more severe disabilities will often need more support.

Progress as a Measure of Quality

Evaluation according to progress assesses the extent to which residents are acquiring the skills perceived to be necessary for participation in activities whose patterns approximate those of the general population. This approach to program evaluation assumes that the acquisition of certain skills will afford a service recipient access to the benefits associated with a high-quality lifestyle. Measures of progress are also future oriented in their reliance on skill acquisition as an indication of the future lifestyle of the service recipient. This orientation toward the future is also apparent in the evaluation of program success based on movement through a defined continuum of residential services (Schalock, Harper, & Genug, 1981). While the results of skill acquisition provide a measure of quality (as far as skills are concerned) they still only indirectly measure the quality of life enjoyed by a service recipient. Current progress measures in common use include the Adaptive Behavior Scales (Nihira, Foster, Shellhass, & Lealand, 1974); the Progress Assessment Chart (Gunzburg, 1977); and the Behavior Development Survey (University of California, Los Angeles, 1979). Some states have developed their own measurement systems directed toward evaluation of resident progress, such as the Client Evaluation Record (CER) (State of Oregon, 1979) and the Developmental Disabilities Information System in New York (Janicki & Jacobson, 1979). Progress measures of program quality offer certain advantages over the capacity measures. Measuring resident skill acquisition is more responsive to programmatic interventions. If a resident is not acquiring new skills, staff may design a new intervention specifically for that resident, whereas it would be difficult to redesign some of the capacity measures for the benefit of one resident, for example, to change the location of the home. Progress measures also offer the advantage of focusing on independence which is one of the valued outcomes for residents. Increasing resident skills is consistent with the developmental programming model. Increasing independence, however, is an uncertain indicator of program quality because once again, the measurement of skill levels is an indirect index of impact on the lifestyle of residents. The acquisition of skills in instructional environments is no guarantee that these same skills will be synthesized into a functional activity by the resident (Brown, Nietupski, & Hamre-Nietupski, 1976). Furthermore, some of these skills prove to be unnecessary, or impossible to acquire, for some residents. In such cases adapted performance strategies provide alternate behavior forms for residents to utilize to achieve the same functional outcome of an activity (Baumgart, Brown, Pumpian, Nisbeth, Ford, Sweet, Messina, & Schroeder, 1982; Brown, Branston, Hamre-Nietupski, Pumpian, Certo, & Gruenewald, 1979; and Whilet, 1980). This over-emphasis on skill acquisition actually presents a disincentive to programs serving residents with more severe or profound disabilities. Programs serving these individuals may not be able to demonstrate progress in either skill acquisition or movement to other levels in the residential continuum. Programs serving more severely disabled residents require alternative ways to measure lifestyles--one that does not assume that achievement of complete independence is the only measure of a high quality lifestyle. Achievement of independence may not even be a realistic goal for many persons with more severe and profound disabilities.

Lifestyle as a Measure of Quality

Some capacity measures are important for preventing atrocities and for measuring some program characteristics on a less frequent basis. Progress measures focus on outcomes to residents. However, neither are adequate indicators of quality in residential services or in the positive impact on lifestyles. These shortcomings are due to the indirect nature of the measures; that is, they never directly examine the lifestyles of the service recipients. In contrast, use of lifestyle measures reduces the level of inference that is built into the capacity and progress measures. A certain level of faith is required to infer that, because a program's environment and procedures demonstrate some capacity for integration, or that a program's residents are gaining new skills, that these residents are therefore experiencing a high-quality lifestyle. If it is agreed that physical integration (engaging in activities outside the home) is a valued feature of a high quality lifestyle, then direct measurement of the number of times a resident engages in such activities is warranted. Capacity measures will reveal, to some degree, the extent to which this may be possible. Progress measures will reveal if a resident knows how to ride buses or cross streets safely, but only the direct examination of the resident's daily activity pattern will demonstrate whether physical integration is being achieved. This measurement strategy also diminishes the single focus on skill acquisition as a measure of quality. Since physical integration provides the level of measurement, more flexibility is afforded to the program and resident as to how this is achieved. Adapted performance strategies or staff support to engage in activities in the community can supplement skill training for residents with more severe disabilities. Since the lifestyle measures focus on current lifestyle, they are appropriate for persons with severe or profound disabilities for whom complete independence is not a current or realistic goal.

Access to a high-quality lifestyle should not be contingent on movement to some higher level of the service continuum or the acquisition of prerequisite skills. The quality of a person's lifestyle is too important to be bargained away on the assumption that it will be better in the future, especially when the future is uncertain or distant. Lifestyle measures afford the opportunity for service consumers, providers, and planners to define not only the features of a normalizing service, but also the normalizing outcomes that service consumers would achieve. The utilization of lifestyle measures in residential programs has been limited to infrequent but exciting possibilities for improving the lifestyles of people with disabilities. Edgerton (1975), and Edgerton & Bercovici (1976) employed a lifestyle measure that might be referred to as "life sharing." In this approach the investigator actually shares in the residential experiences of people with disabilities and reports the results of observations, interviews, and conversations in order to form a picture of the individual's lifestyle. Other authors have collected information on service recipients' lifestyles through structured interviews or self-reports of activity patterns and the nature and extent of community contacts (Dalgleish, 1983; O'Neill, Brown, Gordon, Schonhorn, & Greer, 1981; and Sowers, 1982). Finally, direct observation of people in their residential service settings has been employed by several investigators (Butler & Bjannes, 1978; Landesman-Dwyer, Sackett, & Kleiman, 1980; Landesman-Dwyer, Stein, & Sackett, 1978; and Singer, Close, Irvin, Gersten, & Sailor, 1984). In each case except Singer et al. (1984), discrete units of behavior formed the basis of the coding systems. Singer et al. adapted the Weekly Activity Interview (Sowers, 1982) to directly record the activities engaged in by group home residents. If we agree that measurement of lifestyles may provide an appropriate framework for evaluating the impact of residential programs on the lives of people with disabilities, then the identification of the features of a high-quality lifestyle becomes our next task.

Defining Valued Outcomes of Residential Services

Program design should never proceed without first identifying the values that drive the organization's systems. If an organization's values are to provide the world with an inexpensive supply of food, then perhaps the Nestle Company has done an admirable job. If, however, the values were to provide a source of nutritionally sound food, then Nestle's may have to retool to be in line with these values. Likewise a residential program that values protection of people with disabilities from the dangers of living in our society would be expected to go about its business very differently from a program that values integration and participation in the activities available to the general citizenry. Figure 1 depicts the relationship of values to the issues of program design.

Decision making that is related to a program's values will significantly influence all aspects of the program, such as (1) the design of the technology to achieve these values; (2) the organizational structure that will best facilitate the valued accomplishments; and (3) the information system employed to provide feedback on the program's success. These decisions, to be truly effective, should always be made in reference to what is valued by the organization. Following the earlier example, the program that values protecting its residents from the dangers of society will organize itself to maximize close supervision of residents by regimenting daily routines and providing all necessary services in a closed and isolated environment. The technology will maximize the control of resident access to activities and people, and the information system will focus on the reporting of incidents that have endangered residents. In contrast the program that values integration and participation will organize itself to be

```
                          VALUES
                            |
                            v
                        OUTCOME
                        MEASURES

    TECHNOLOGY                          INFO SYSTEM


                      ORGANIZATION
```

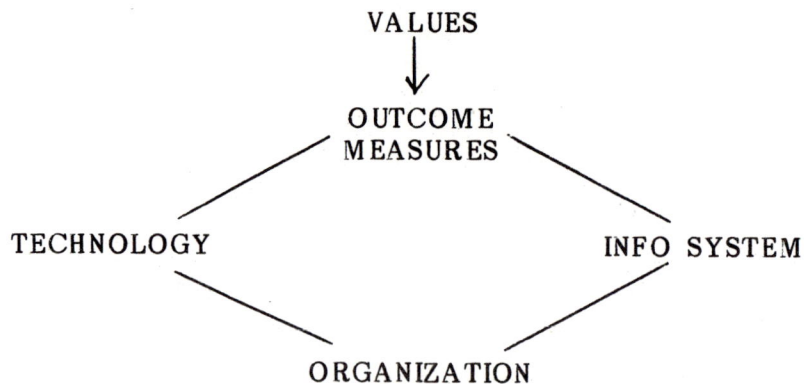

Figure 1.
Relationship of values to program design.

in close proximity to community resources and other members of the community. It will employ a technology that teaches people to become more competent in accessing their community and developing social networks, and its information system will provide feedback regarding the extent to which service recipients are participating in community activities.

The determination of residential service values proceeds by examining the valued outcomes desired by three groups of people: the service consumers, the parents/advocates of people with disabilities, and the service providers. Several authors have emphasized the need to address quality of life in program evaluations (Bruininks & Lakin, 1985; Emerson, 1985; and Heal, Sigleman, & Switzky, 1978). Quality of life has been defined in terms of physical integration in the community (Zigler & Balla, 1977), and social integration (Balla & Klein, 1981; Heal et al., 1978; and Janicki, 1981). Willer and Intagliata (1984) stress the need for quality of life measures in addition to the more traditional focus on developing independent living skills. Zigler and Balla (1977) further state that "any comprehensive program of research must take into account not only the behavioral functioning of residents but the quality of life they experience [and] the extent to which they maintain contact with the community . . ." (p. 10). Input from parents/advocates, service consumers and residential service providers was gathered through the efforts of the Neighborhood Living Project, a joint research and development effort of the University of Oregon's Specialized Training Program and the State of Washington's Division of Developmental Disabilities (Newton, Boles, Romer, Bellamy, & Horner, 1985). This information was used in the design of the Neighborhood Living Model which will be described further in the next section of this paper. Additional information on the outcomes that would be valued in residential programs was available from the State of Washington's Division of Developmental Disabilities Residential Services Outcomes Task Force which was also made up of parents of people with disabilities and residential service consumers and providers. The Task Force was charged with the task of developing guidelines for the measurement of those outcomes that were to be valued in residential programs which contracted to provide such services in the State of Washington. This process resulted in the inclusion of five values in the Neighborhood Living Model: physical integration, social integration, variety of activities, independence in performing activities, and security. Table 1 provides the operational definitions of these valued outcomes. Other outcomes valued in residential services were identified but are not currently included in any measurement system. These values include choice in one's lifestyle and health. Provisions are included in the Neighborhood Living Model to address these values, but they are still capacity or progress measures. Plans are being developed to define them as outcomes and build measures for these values.

Table 1.
Lifestyle Outcome Measures.

Outcome	Measure
1. Physical Integration	The number of activities performed outside the property boundary of the home (or communal areas of an apartment).
2. Social Integration	The number of activities performed with individuals who are not (a) staff members, (b) persons paid to work with individuals with developmental disabilities, or (c) other residents. Separate brief contacts, extended contacts, contacts with significant others.
3. Variety	The number of different categories of activities performed within a given time period (week, month, etc.).
4. Independence	The number of valued activities performed without staff assistance.
5. Security	The number of months of continuous support without forced movement to a restrictive setting.

Measuring Valued Outcomes in Residential Services

The remainer of this paper describes a measurement system designed to assess the lifestyles of persons with moderate, severe or profound disabilities who receive 24-hour residential support services. This measurement system was developed as part of the Neighborhood Living Model.

The Neighborhood Living Model is a comprehensive set of systems for integrating eight or fewer people with severe disabilities into their local communities. The model was developed to have a meaningful impact on the lifestyles of residents. There are four important components to the model: (1) the values that have been used to guide development of model procedures, (2) an internal data system that measures the lifestyles of residents, (3) a training and intervention technology that helps residents to gain and maintain adaptive behavior, and (4) an organizational structure that promotes program longevity and effectiveness. This internal data system forms one component of a comprehensive approach to program evaluation. Some elements of program quality would be difficult to measure on a repeated basis within a residential service setting. Elements such as program size and location, respect for residents, and privacy should still be assessed through periodic evaluation from persons or agencies external to the service program setting. Some of the previously discussed evaluation strategies can be employed for this purpose. The Valued Outcomes Information System (VOIS), which forms the internal data system, addresses itself to examining those indicators that were determined to index the quality of life experienced by service recipients.

Development of the internal data system was guided by six characteristics felt to be fundamental for any system to be useful to consumers, service providers and parents/advocates. These characteristics included the following:

1. Data should be tied to valued events in a service recipient's daily life.
2. Data system should be simple to use, that is take no more than a two-day inservice to learn.
3. Data should not require more than 5% of total staff time for collection and summarization.

4. Data should be valid and reliable.
5. Data should be used for decision making.
6. Program staff should not require continued external support to operate the system.

The requirement that data be tied to valued events was addressed by the decision to use activities as the unit of organization for the data collection system. Wilcox and Bellamy (1982) presented the rationale for using activities as a unit of analysis, as opposed to skills or other discrete units of behavior. They defined activities as age appropriate, functional units of behavior that create natural consequences in a person's life. Using a public telephone, going to the bank, and purchasing groceries are activities; identifying numbers, signing one's name and counting change are skills. An activity is made up of an integrated set of skills that result in a functional outcome that may be maintained by the consequences of the activity. In order to categorize activities into a system that would allow for ease in tracking daily patterns of valued events, an activity catalog was developed for use in residential settings (Bellamy & Wilcox, in press). This catalog consists of some 170 activities that are available in the local communities where residential services are provided. Each local program has the option of adding activities to the catalog that are unique to the community. The catalog consists of two domains--Personal Management and Leisure. Each of these domains is further divided into categories such as media, exercise, games, crafts and hobbies, and events, in the Leisure domain; and self, food, space and belongings, and personal business in the Personal Management domain. Each activitiy has a unique 3-digit code. For example, going to a movie is 1.4.3, which indicates that it is 1, in the Leisure domain; 4, in the category of events; and 3, attending a movie. While this may sound complicated at first, in fact, staff of residential programs using this system quickly become familiar with the most commonly encountered activities.

Once activities were defined as the unit of organization, rules were developed regarding which activities should be recorded. Any activity that is physically integrated, that is, occurs outside the property boundaries of the home, and any activity that is socially integrated, that is, is accompanied by someone other than staff or other residents, is considered to be a valued lifestyle indicator and is therefore recorded for all residents. Other activities that are of unique interest or importance to a specific resident are targeted as objectives in the IHP process and recorded whenever they occur. These activities are selected by the resident, parents/advocates and staff for either training (increasing the level of independence) or as participation activities (no current objective for training but some specified level of performance opportunity is guaranteed in the IHP process). Participation activities are those that are important to the resident's lifestyle but are not targeted for an increased level of independence. Staff provide whatever scheduling and support is necessary to achieve the specified level of performance opportunities.

Data are gathered through the use of small-size Post-It notes that are imprinted with a template to record the following: the resident's name, who accompanied the resident, what the activity was, when it occurred, where it occurred (home or community), whether it contained social integration, and whether training occurrred (whether task analysis data were collected). These tags are then summarized on a weekly basis by staff. Lifestyle graphs are then constructed showing the proportion of activities that were socially integrated, physically integrated and contained training. Figure 2 is a representation of a lifestyle graph for one resident.

The top line of the lifestyle graph labeled social integration indicates the total number of valued activities performed by the resident each week. The total includes all activities that were either physically integrated, socially integrated or were listed as an objective on the resident's IHP. The area labled As on the graph, between the top line and the line below it, are all the activities that did not involve social integration for this resident. The areas labeled P, Ap, and So together represent all the activities that involved social integration for this resident. The P area represents the activities

Lifestyle graphs

Physical Integration　　　　　　　　　　　　　**(Mary)**

Community

Home

Social Integration

As

P

AP

SO

Training & Other

Everything
Else

Training

NUMBER OF ACTIVITIES

WEEKS

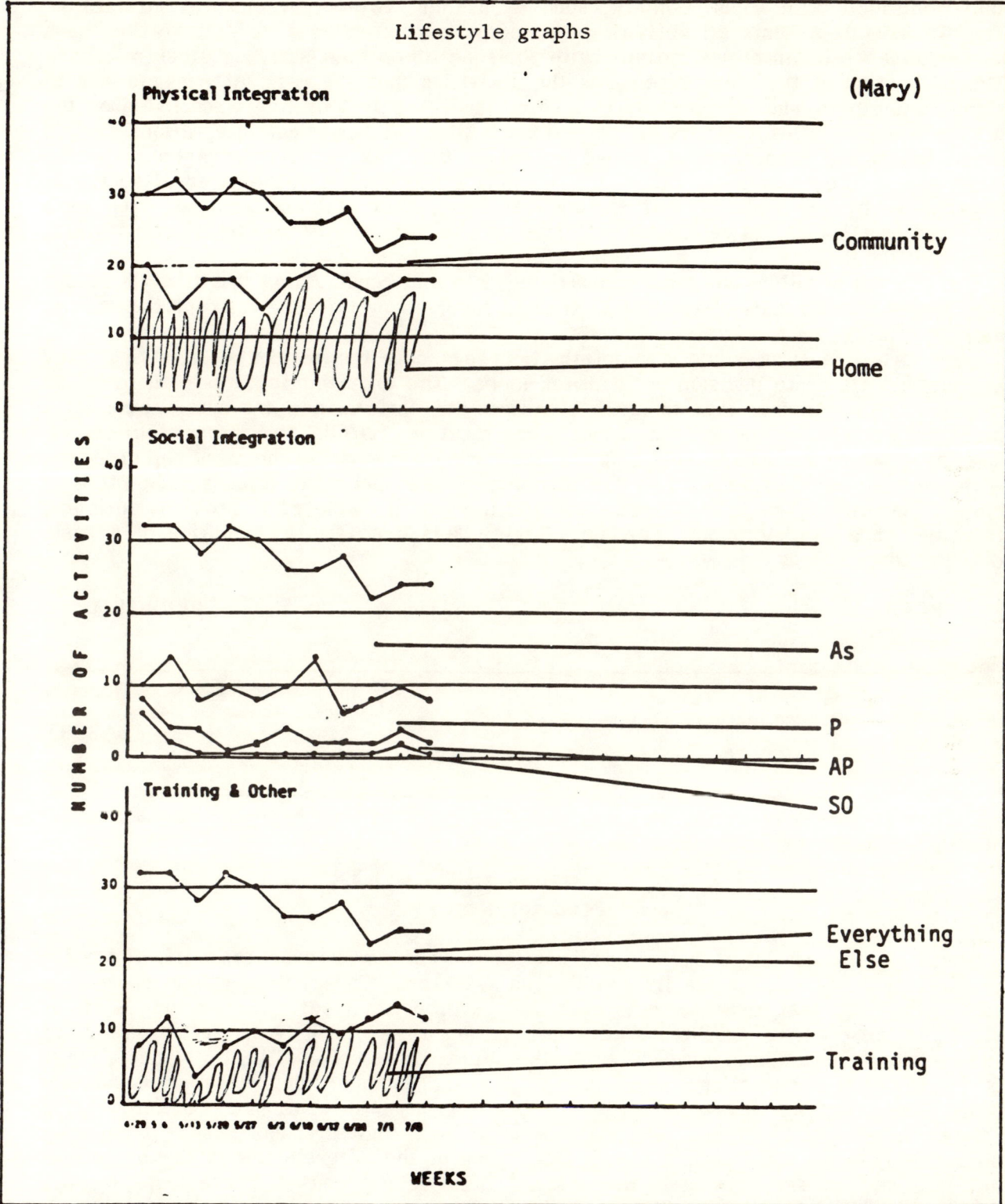

Figure 2.
Resident (Mary) lifestyle graphs.

19

that contained brief social contact, such as a short two-way reciprocal interaction. The Ap area represents all activities that contained extended social integration, such as performance of an entire activity with someone other than staff or other residents. The So portion of the graph represents the activities that the resident engaged in with significant others, such as members of his/her family or persons who were listed on the IHP as being significant others in the resident's life. The physical integration lifestyle graph shows the proportion of valued activities that the resident engaged in in the home and in the community. Last, the training graph depicts the number of activities engaged in by the resident that included training, that is, task analysis data were gathered by staff on the resident's performance and the activity was listed as a training objective on the IHP.

The process of filling out tags, summarizing data and constructing the lifestyle graphs took about 2.5% to 3.5% of total staff time as reported by the nine residential programs currently using the VOIS.

Once data are summarized into information regarding the residents' lifestyles, they are incorporated into decision or feedback loops. The essential features of a feedback loop are (1) a planning stage in which standards for performance are established; (2) a performing stage in which the service organization fulfulls its responsibilities; (3) measuring, which includes summarizing the data; and (4) comparing the measured outcomes with the standards established in the planning stage. Once the loop is completed, or closed, the planning stage is entered again and the loop is employed to provide continuing feedback on a predetermined schedule. Figure 3 is a schematic rendition of a basic decision loop.

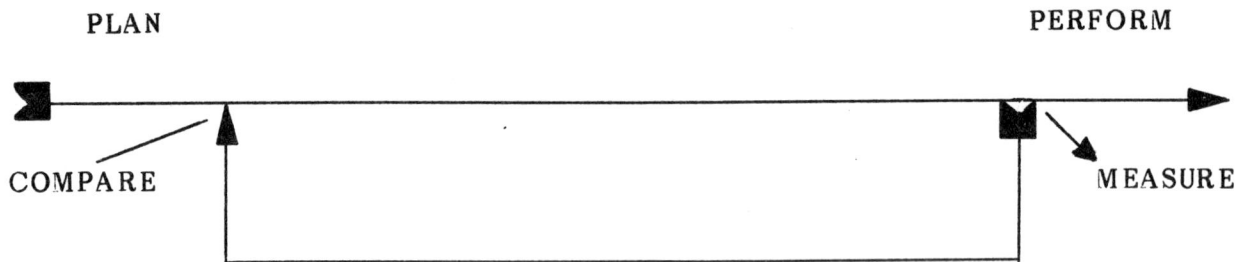

PLAN   PERFORM

COMPARE   MEASURE

Figure 3.
Feedback loop.

The VOIS employs three distinct decision loops: consumer/advocate, staff, and board of directors. Each loop has its own unique features. The consumer loop runs on a six-month cycle that coincides with each IHP development meeting. This loop contains plans for the lifestyle measures of the resident on a six-month basis, the summary for the six-month period, and comparisons to the standards established in the planning stage of the previous IHP meeting. The board of directors decision loop closes on a monthly basis. The program's director provides the board with monthly summaries of information related to resident lifestyles. The staff decision loop, logically, closes more frequently on a weekly basis. This permits timely monitoring of the progress toward IHP objectives and informed decision making in the area of lifestyle outcomes. These loops support answers to questions regarding the extent of physical and social integration in a resident's lifestyle and the degree to which training occurred. Outcome measures of variety of activities and independence are computed using the activity catalog and incorporated into the decision loops of the consumer and the board of directors. These measures assess variety by examining the distribution of activities across categories and independence by asking staff to rate the level of support residents have received for engaging in the activities contained in the catalog.

The VOIS is currently in use in eight residential service programs in the state of Washington and in one program in Alaska. These programs include five Intensive Tenant Support programs providing services, in their apartments, to individuals with moderate to severe disabilities, three group homes, and an adult family (foster) home. A total of 58 residents are served through these programs, all of whom have moderate or severe disabilities.

Conclusions

The VOIS is one way to examine the lifestyles of persons with disabilities for the purposes of evaluating and designing residential services. This system will be expanded over time to include other important features of quality in lifestyles. Distinct advantages in using the VOIS over other measures of quality in residential programs include the removal of the high level of inference regarding actual lifestyles, which is inherent in the capacity and progress measures; the opportunity for service consumers and their parents/advocates to make better informed choices about where a person may choose to live; and the fact that while the VOIS defines the framework for lifestyle measurement it does not dictate what a lifestyle should be for individuals. This last advantage in the VOIS allows for informed lifestyle planning involving the service consumer and the significant others in his/her life (O'Brien, in press). However, the most important feature of the VOIS is that it defines what we value as outcomes of our residential service programs. We currently debate the need for more staff in residential programs, technical assistance to programs, the effect of size in our programs, the level of skills needed by staff and how to best develop these skills. What we lack is a viable method to determine the impact these various interventions have on the quality of residential service. The VOIS, and other measures of lifestyle that can be employed at the service delivery level, allow us to assess this impact where it is most critical, on the lifestyles of the people receiving services. No amount of research will validate normalization and deinstitutionalization as valued goals, nor will research provide us with the answers to what should be the outcomes of quality residential services. Our ideals and our goals are value decisions and are not subject to validation through the scientific method. Research is essential to develop strategies and tactics for improving the quality of our services. But first, we must know what quality is.

References

Balla, D. H., & Klein, M. S. (1981). Labels for and taxonomies of environments for retarded persons. In H. C. Haywood & J. R. Newbrough (Eds.), Living environments for developmentally retarded persons (pp. 3-14). Baltimore: University Park Press.

Bank-Mikkelson, N. E. (1969). A metropolitan area in Denmark: Copenhagen. In R. Kugel & W. Wolfensberger (Eds.), Changing patterns in residential services for the mentally retarded (pp. 227-254). Washington, D.C.: President's Committee on Mental Retardation.

Baumgart, D., Brown, L., Pumpian, I., Nisbet, J., Ford, A. Sweet, M., Messina, R., & Schroeder, J. (1982). Principle of partial participation and individualized adaptations in educational programs for severely handicapped students. Journal of the Association for the Severely Handicapped, 7, 17-27.

Bellamy, G. T., Newton, J. S., & Lebaron, N. (1985). Toward lifestyle accountability in residential services for persons with mental retardation. Unpublished manuscript, University of Oregon, Specialized Training Program, Eugene.

Bellamy, G. T., & Wilcox, B. (Eds.). (In press). The activities catalog: A community programming guide for youth and adults with severe disabilities. Baltimore: Paul H. Brookes.

Behavior Development Survey User's Manual (1979). Pmona, CA: University of California, Los Angeles, Neuropsychiatric Institute Research Group at Lanterman State Hospital.

Brown, L., Branston, M. B., Hamre-Nietupski, S., Pumpian, I., Certo, N., & Greunewald, L. (1979). A strategy for developing chronological-age-appropriate and functional curricular contents for severely handicapped adolescents and young adults. Journal of Special Education, 13, 81-90.

Brown, L., Nietupski, J., & Hamre-Nietupski, S. (1976). The criterion of ultimate functioning. In Hey, don't forget about me: New directions for serving the severely handicapped (pp. 2-15). Reston, VA: Council for Exceptional Children.

Bruininks, R. H., & Lakin, K. C. (1985). Perspective and prospects for social and educational integration. In R. H. Bruininks & K. C. Lakin (Eds.), Living and learning in the least restrictive environment (pp. 253-277). Baltimore: Paul H. Brookes.

Butler, E. W., & Bjannes, A. T. (1978). Activities and use of time by retarded persons in community care facilities. In G. P. Sackett (Ed.), Observing behavior, Vol. 1: Theory and applications in mental retardation (pp. 379-399). Baltimore: University Park Press.

Dalgleish, M. (1983). Assessments of residential environments for mentally retarded adults in Britain. Mental Retardation, 21, 204-208.

Division of Developmental Disabilities. (1985). Residential Services Guidelines. Olympia, WA.

Edgerton, R. B. (1975). Issues relating to the quality of life among mentally retarded persons. In M. J. Begab & S. A. Richardson (Eds.), The mentally retarded and society: A social science perspective (pp. 127-140). Baltimore: University Park Press.

Edgerton, R. B., & Bercovici, S. M. (1976). The cloak of competence: Years later. American Journal of Mental Deficiency, 80, 485-497.

Emerson, E. B. (1985). Evaluating the impact of deinstitutionalization on the lives of mentally retarded people. American Journal of Mental Deficiency, 90, 227-288.

Goffman, E. (1961). Asylums. Garden City, New York: Anchor Books.

Gunzburg, H. C. (1977). Progress assessment chart of social and personal development (5th Ed.). Stratford upon Avon, England: SEFA Publications, Ltd.

Gunzburg, H. C., & Gunzburg, A. L. (1973). 39 steps leading towards normalized living practices in living units for the mentally handicapped. British Journal on Mental Subnormality, 19, 91-99.

Hauber, F. A., Bruininks, R. H., Hill, B. K., Lakin, K. C., Scheerenberger, R. C., & White, C. C. (1984). National census of residential facilities: A 1982 profile of facilities and residents. American Journal of Mental Deficiency, 89, 236-245.

Heal, L. W., Sigelman, C. K., & Switzky, H. N. (1978). Research on community residential alternatives for the mentally retarded. In N. R. Ellis (Ed.), International review of research in mental retardation (Vol. 9, pp. 209-249). New York: Academic Press.

Hill, B. K., Lakin, K. C., & Bruininks, R. H. (1984). Trends in residential services for people who are mentally retarded: 1972-1982. The Journal of the Association for Persons with Severe Handicaps, 9, 243-250.

Janicki, M. P. (1981). Personal growth and community residence environments: A review. In H. C. Haywood & J. R. Newbrough (Eds.), Living environments for developmentally retarded persons (pp. 59-101). Baltimore: University Park Press.

Janicki, M. P., & Jacobson, J. W. (1979). New York's needs assessment and developmental disabilities: Preliminary report (Technical Monograph 79-100). Albany, New York: New York State Office of Mental Retardation and Developmental Disabilities.

King, R. D., Raynes, N. V., & Tizard, J. (1971). Patterns of residential care: Sociological studies in institutions for handicapped children. London: Routledge & Kegan Paul.

Landesman-Dwyer, S., Sackett, G. P., & Kleinman, J. S. (1980). Relationship of size to resident and staff behavior in small community residencies. American Journal of Mental Deficiency, 85, 6-17.

Landesman-Dwyer, S., Stein, J. G., & Sackett, G. P. (1978). A behavioral and ecological study of group homes. In G. P. Sackett (Ed.), Observing behavior, Volume 1: Theory and applications in mental retardation (pp. 349-378). Baltimore: University Park Press.

MacEachron, A. E. (1983). Institutional reform and adaptive functioning of mentally retarded persons: A field experiment. American Journal of Mental Deficiency, 88. 2-12.

Mental Health Division (1979). Client evaluation record. Salem, OR: Author.

Moos, R., & Lemke, S. (1979). The multiphasic environmental assessment procedure (MEAP): Preliminary manual (report no. or similar if there is one). Palo Alto, CA: Standord University and VA Medical Center, Social Ecology Laboratory.

Morris, P. (1969). Put away: A sociological study of institutions for the mentally retarded. New York: Atherton.

Newton, J. S., Boles, S., Romer, M., Bellamy, G. T., & Horner, R. H. (1985). Final report: Deinstitutionaliation models for severely handicapped children and youth (Grant No. 300-81-0406). Eugene, OR: University of Oregon, Specialized Training Program.

Nihira, K., Foster, R., Shellhaas, M., & Lealand, H. (1974). Adaptive Behavior Scale: Manual. Washington, D.C.: American Association of Mental Deficiency.

Nirje, B. (1969). The normalization principle and its human management implications. In R. Kugel & W. Wolfensberger (Eds.), Changing patterns in residential services for the mentally retarded (pp. 179-195). Washington, D.C.: President's Committee on Mental Retardation.

O'Brien, J. (In Press). A guide to lifestyle planning. In G. T. Bellamy & B. Wilcox (Eds.), The activities catalog: A community programming guide for youth and adults with severe disabilities. Baltimore: Paul H. Brookes.

O'Neill, J., Brown, M., Gordon, W., Schonhorn, R., & Greer, E. (1981). Activity patterns of mentally retarded adults in institutions and communities: A longitudinal study. Applied Research in Mental Retardation, 2, 367-379.

Pratt, M. W., Luszea, M. A., & Brown, M. E. (1980). Measuring dimensions of the quality of care in small community residences. American Journal of Mental Deficiency, 85, 188-194.

Schalock, R. L., Harper, R. S., & Genung, T. (1981). Community integration of mentally retarded adults: Community placement and program success. American Journal of Mental Deficiency, 85, 478-488.

Singer, G. H. S., Close, D. W., Irvin, L. K., Gersten, R., & Sailor, W. (1984). An alternative to the institution for young people with severely handicapping conditions in a rural community. The Journal of the Association for Persons with Severe Handicaps, 9, 231-261.

Sowers, J. (1982). Validation of the weekly activity interview (WHI): An instrument designed to measure the lifestyle of severely handicapped secondary-age students. Unpublished doctoral dissertation, University of Oregon, Department of Rehabilitation and Special Education, Eugene, OR.

White, O. R. (1980). Adaptive performance objectives: Form versus function, In W. Sailor, B. Wilcox & L. Brown (Eds.), Methods of instruction for severely handicapped students (pp. 47-69). Baltimore: Paul H. Brookes.

Wilcox, B., & Bellamy, G. T. (1982). Design of high school programs for severely handicapped students. Baltimore: Paul H. Brookes.

Willer, B., & Intagliata, J. (1984). An overview of social policy of deinstitutionalization. In N. R. Ellis & N. W. Bray (Eds.), International review of research in mental retardation (Vol. 13, pp. 1-23). New York: Academic Press.

Wolfensberger, W. (1972). The principle of normalization in human services. Toronto: National Institute on Mental Retardation.

Wolfensberger, W. (1980). The definition of normalization: Update, problems, disagreements, and misunderstandings. In R. J. Flynn & K. E. Nitsch (eds.), Normalization, social integration, and community services (pp. 71-115). Baltimore: University Park Press.

Wolfensberger, W., & Glenn, L. (1975). PHSS 3, a method for quantitative evaluation of human services. Toronto: National Institute on Mental Retardation.

Wolfensberger, W., & Thomas, S. (1983). PASSING (program analysis of service systems implementation of normalization goals): Normalization criteria and ratings manual (2nd ed.). Toronto: National Institute on Mental Retardation.

Zigler, E., & Balla, D. A. (1977). Impact of institutional experience on the behavior and development of retarded persons. American Journal of Mental Deficiency, 82, 1-11.

In Response to Lyle T. Romer

A Systems Approach to Quality Residential Services for
Those Who Are Profoundly Handicapped with Deafness and Blindness

George H. S. Singer

Introduction

This conference has been called in order to develop recommendations based upon the needs of students with handicaps of deafness and blindness who are leaving school services and entering the adult service system. Our emphasis is on transition to adult services of those individuals who experience deaf-blindness and other profound, multiple handicapping conditions. This session is concerned with residential alternatives. In this context I would like to comment briefly on Lyle Romer's excellent paper and then discuss some of the implications of serving individuals who exhibit severe aberrant behavior in community living arrangements. Because our context is broad, covering service needs and policy implications, this paper will discuss several issues. I will first talk about what we hope to achieve for young adults who are severely handicapped and then discuss some of the policies, community services, and organizational characteristics that are required in order to create desirable homes. I will talk about several layers of the service system, starting with the daily schedule and social interactions of a person who experiences deaf-blindness. I will then move on to discuss the organization that provides home-living services, and then on to some of the essential community services that are required to create successful living arrangements. And finally, I will talk about some of the federal and state policies that have a decisive impact on the quality of daily life of individuals who experience severely handicapping conditions.

The Person Who Is Profoundly/Multiply Handicapped
with Deaf-Blindness: A Description

The population of those who are deaf-blind, like the larger population of severely handicapped individuals, is extremely heterogeneous. This discussion will be focusing on individuals who experience deafness and blindness in addition to severe to profound mental retardation. A large percentage of these young people experience additional handicapping conditions including cerebral palsy, epilepsy, and other chronic medical conditions. Many of these individuals will leave school without having learned a symbolic communication system; those who have learned a symbolic system will have a very limited linguistic repertoire. A significant number of these young people will exhibit severe aberrant behaviors, one of the primary causes of first placements and returns to institutions and, ostensibly, one of the main obstacles to placing individuals in the community (Hill, Lakin, & Bruinincks, 1984). The problem behaviors that are associated with institutionalization are self-injurious behavior, assaultive behavior, severe noncompliance, and destruction of property (Scheerenberger, 1981). Thus a discussion of community living for these individuals needs to take into account their need for several services including behavioral and medical treatment. The challenge is to meet these service needs in a homelike setting and in the context of a positive and culturally normal lifestyle.

Where Do They Live Now?

The majority of adults with profound/multiple handicaps of deaf-blindness are residing in institutions—public residential institutions and private nursing homes (Wolf, Delk, & Schein, 1982). Until recently, the institution has been the expected place of residence for these individuals. As a result, a majority of these adults reside in large public institutions, and many who live in the community reside in nursing homes and other mini-institutions (Wolf et al., 1982, Lakin, Hill, Hauber, & Bruininks, 1983). Needless to say, these are not homelike settings. The situation is different for the school-aged population. A recent survey of nine Rocky Mountain and Great Plains states showed that 38% of school-aged children who are deaf-blind were residing in institutions, 18% in residential schools, and the remaining 44% in community settings (Gates, 1985). Another recent study from New York state suggests a similar pattern. Although they did not provide specific information about children with deaf-blindness, Jacobson & Janicki (1985) did describe the living arrangements for children with multiple handicapping conditions and profound mental retardation. They found that twice as many frail/severely handicapped individuals, aged 21 or less, lived in the community as compared with the institution. The opposite was true of adults; only one in three lived in the community. It appears that many children are living in natural or foster homes and their parents expect that they can and will continue to live in community homes rather than institutions. But this outcome is by no means ensured. The prognosis for full community services for all persons regardless of the severity of their handicapping conditions is, at best, guarded.

On one hand, funding has continued to favor institutions and large facilities rather than homes (Fernald, 1986). Many people have been left in the large congregate-care institutions and many others have been transferred from one institution to a another in the community (Taylor, McCord, & Searl, 1981). And, sadly, some individuals have been placed in homes that are underfunded and insufficiently staffed, thereby creating "back wards" in the community (Bercovici, 1981). On the other hand, several states have aggressively created small group homes, apartment-living programs, and small scale ICF-MR home (Apolloni, 1980; Hitzing, 1980). Empirical evidence suggests that these community-living arrangements create new opportunities for growth in adaptive skills and for more normative, valued lifestyles (Conroy, Efthimious, & Lemanowiscz, 1982; Romer, 1986). Deinstitutionalization has proceeded at a rate of about 6,000 placements in the community each year with the recent movement made up mostly of individuals with severe and profound mental retardation. At the same time there is a growing number of new community homes for individuals who have lived in the community their entire lives. As we serve more severely handicapped persons in larger numbers in the community, the issue of how to create homes for individuals with severe aberrant behaviors has become prominent.

On the positive side, there are now examples of excellent service models in several states. (Apolloni, Cappuccilli, & Cooke, 1980; Gage, Fredericks, Baldwin, Moore, & Grove, 1979; Singer, Close, Irvin, Gersten, & Sailor, 1984; Romer, 1986). However, the idea of community living in small homelike settings is relatively new and fragile, particularly for the group that concerns us here today. The community service system in most states has yet to develop homelike residences for medically frail individuals, people with severe aberrant behaviors, and people with multiple developmental special needs. If we want to create family-like homes for this group of people there are several service system components that must be in place. I believe that we can serve all individuals in positive family-like settings given adequate resources, sufficient community services, local leadership, and a clear understanding of our goal.

The Goal: A Positive Quality of Life

It is important to have a clear sense of the desired outcomes of the service system. In the most general sense, we want to provide a positive quality of life for the people we serve. The concept of quality of life as it is used in our field usually refers to one person's surmise of what life is like for someone who cannot speak for him - or herself. It would be a lot easier to agree on what makes a high quality service if we could simply ask our clients, "How's life?" For example, a recent study of semi-independent living programs for individuals with mild mental retardation relied extensively on interviews with the residents (Halpern, Close, & Walker, 1985). They spoke with considerable agreement about the sources of satisfaction and the troubles in their lives. With this kind of information, we might agree that a residential program that increased those sources of satisfaction and decreased the troublesome events would be improving a person's quality of life. The problem is more difficult though, when we have to make inferences about what life is like for a person who cannot easily revel how s/he feels and what s/he prefers.

Instead of asking, we have to resort to observing. But what to observe? Researchers such as Close (1977) have tended to emphasize skill development. Gaining new skills plausibly gives access to more independent participation in activities of daily living. Learning new skills has something to do with a good quality of life although we probably all know successful students who are unhappy and people who do not learn lots of new skills who say they are satisfied. And certainly too much emphasis on skill development might put people in a kind of pressure cooker instead of a home.

Social reformers such as Wolfensberger and Glenn (1975) have tended to emphasize the normalcy of the physical and social environment—the location of home, its proximity to stores and transportation, the amount of space and personal possessions for each resident in the home, the daily routine of the residents, the appropriateness of programming, and so on. These normalization dimensions probably have something to do with what most people associate with a good quality of life. However, we probably all know people who live in nice homes, have a normal rhythm of life, and still aren't happy.

Romer and his colleagues have added a more specific dimension of normalization by evaluating the frequency of valued activities and of social contacts. From this point of view, a service that delivers a high quality of life is one that creates a valued lifestyle made up of activities in integrated community settings.

So far, all of these ways of looking at quality of life direct attention to measurable outcomes of a social service and, on the face of it, seem to point to aspects of what many people would consider to be a good life. Quality of life is a concept with many dimensions and we probably get closest to measuring it by looking at it from several different angles. In addition to looking at skill gains, normalization of the social and physical environment, and valued activities, I think that we need to look at the people whom we serve from two other points of view by asking two more questions: (a) How do the people who spend the most time with them treat them? and (b) Do they seem happy?

Remember, I am talking about people who need a lot of assistance to participate in normal activities of daily living. This means that someone--a friend, relative, foster parent, or group home employee is spending a lot of time in close contact with the individual. Research from the studies of depression and well-being with nonhandicapped people suggests that the quality of our close social contacts at work and at home has a lot to do with our morale (Cohen & Syme, 1984). The quality of caregiver/resident social interactions have been a major concern in institutions and poor quality community residences (Bogdan, Taylor, Grandpre, & Haynes, 1977; Bercovici, 1981). We are all familiar with reports of disrespect, disdain, and abuse. However, little attention has been paid to social interactions between caregivers and residents in good living environments. I would expect them to be characterized by two-way communication in which the individual who is deaf-blind not only receives but also initiates communication during dyadic interactions. Caregivers in high quality homes should be able to comprehend the expressive communications of their residents who are deaf-blind whether these are prelinguistic gestures, manual signs, or even states of alertness. Similary caregivers should communicate frequently about ongoing events--describing, commenting, and turn-taking. Many of these interactions would be characterized by good humor, gentlenes, and candor. And if an aberrant behavior is part of the communication, the staff person would respond with precision, correct technique, and an understanding of the function of the behavior in that specific context.

The second question I would ask about a resident of a community home is "Does s/he seem to be happy?" I am well aware of what a sloppy, slippery construct is at hand. If persons cannot tell you how they are feeling and if their nonverbal expressions are not part of the generally consensual nonverbal code of the culture, how do you know? Can we tell how severely handicapped people are feeling in different situations? Some efforts have been made to study social interaction in integrated school settings. These efforts should be extended to community living arrangements. We might need to further individualize this kind of assessment in order to include measures of affect. One approach would be to ask parents or caregivers who know a person very well to tell us when they think the individual is happy. A picture or videotaped record of some of these occasions could serve as a standard. A guardian, advocate, or program evaluator could observe a resident on several occasions and ask how often the deaf/blind individual looks like s/he did in the pictures that showed a happy state. Of course, other "harder" behavioral measures and indices such as rates of aberrant behavior, requests for continuation of an event, and attending to the environment would need to be considered.

An Example

I want to tell a brief story to indicate why the questions, "How do others treat the person?" and "How happy are they?" ought to be considered. I was recently asked to serve as an expert witness in efforts to mediate a dispute between a parent and a state department of education. The parent was alleging that her daughter's foster home and school placement were inappropriate. I was asked to evaluate both the educational and residential services that were being provided to Jill, a teenager who was handicapped with deafness and blindness. Jill has been totally blind as well as profoundly deaf since birth. According to her school records, she knew a few difficult-to-read manual signs and could understand a small number of signs made in her hand. Jill's mother felt that the foster home was highly inappropriate, even damaging. I asked that the foster parent keep a diary of the young woman's activities in the foster home and in the community. I also used a normalization instrument to assess the home and social environment. The home was a new, large apartment across the street from the beach. The young woman had her own attractive room; she often went out with the family and played with the other teenager in the home. I watched her and the foster parent at home and at the beach. She behaved like many severely or profoundly mentally retarded people whom I know in that she was very passive. She never made efforts to communicate, did not initiate any activity without prompts, and seemed generally unaware of the environment. I observed her in her respite care program and classroom, where she behaved in much the same way.

Everybody was fed up with Jill's mother and I was beginning to wonder if maybe she had some unreasonable expectations. I met with the mother and we drove to a supermarket in her beat-up old car. All of a sudden, Jill came to life in the car. She started signing into her mother's hands, asking where we were going and what was for dinner. In the store, the guardian asked her to get some lettuce; the young woman who is totally blind felt the produce, found a head of lettuce, found her way back to the cart, put it in and signed "mom's lettuce." Next she asked for cashews by spelling the word. Back at her mother's home which was not nearly as well furnished, spacious, or clean as the foster parent's home, Jill helped with some parts of cooking dinner, asked to go play a game, came back and started a two-way exchange with her mother.

So, here were two contrasting environments. A foster home that seemed to provide "the good life." The location, the possessions, the activities all looked good. Her natural mother's home was more crowded, less attractive, and much further from the beach. But in the foster home, as well as the respite and classroom settings, Jill was largely ignored. People rarely tried to communicate to her, nor did they ever set up interactions that would prompt her to initiate communication. They expected her to be passive and uncommunicative. With her mother, she was a very different person. The interactions between the two women were very different in Jill's mother's home. And Jill looked happier, although her expressions were not conventional and took some time to learn.

Perhaps we are overlooking something. Clearly all of the things that were targeted in our Project S.A.I.L. homes such as skill development, a normalized schedule, activities in the community, and reductions in problem behavior were important (Singer, 1986). Clearly, the outcome measure that Lyle Romer has discussed is extremely important and represents a real contribution to our field. However, we should not shy away from more difficult to measure, but extremely important, indicators of quality of life.

The purpose of this discussion of quality of life indicators is to arrive at an understanding of what we want to create when we make living arrangements for severely handicapped individuals. I am assuming that we want to create living environments that do several things: increase skills, decrease aberrant behaviors, provide normal homelike surroundings, provide a schedule of valued activities, provide positive social interactions, and provide many occasions for happiness. I also assume that at different times these subgoals will be given different degrees of importance. For a person who injures himself, we may, for a time, have to give priority to decreasing the problem behavior over the schedule of community events. There may be times when skill development really matters when, for example, a new job opportunity comes along and a new skill would make placement possible. But each subgoal, at any one time, should be given some care and attention.

What do we need to do to create living environments where we can achieve these goals? And furthermore, what else do we need to do if a person exhibits serious aberrant behaviors?

Components of a Necessary Service System

In the service system, many things must happen on several different societal levels ranging from federal and state law to staff training practices. It is a complex system with many interacting components. Ultimately, we measure the success of each service component by looking at an individual's quality of life. I have listed them in Table 1. To simplify, I have grouped the service components into domains.

Table 1.

State and National

- Philosophy
- Policy
- Funding

Community Services

- Case management
- Guardianship and advocacy
- Generic services

Organizational Variables

- Philosophy
- Governance
- Leadership
- Cohesiveness
- Boundary management
- Routine management
- Personnel management
- Social norms
- Problem resolution
- Planning and evaluation

Individual's Experience of Residential Service

- Activities
- Social interactions
- I.P.P. goals
- Attractiveness and accessibility of home

Individual's Experience

The first domain concerns the individual. There are several elements that come into view at this individual level on analysis such as a person's schedule of activities, social interactions, health, the presence of stressors, skills, individual program plan goals, and the attractiveness and accessibility of the environment.

Organizational Variables

The next level up in the system has to do with the immediate, most proximate determinants of success of the personal level variables. In group-home and apartment-living programs, this level primarily consists of organizational variables. The characteristics of the service organization are primary determinants of the quality at the personal level. Just as the first level is made up of several elements that add up to individual program quality, so the second level consists of many variables that make up organizational effectiveness.

The daily life of a severely handicapped person is largely, but not entirely, determined by the quality of the organization that is providing a particular service. As much as any group of people in our society, severely handicapped people are at the mercy of the organizations that house, clothe, educate, employ, and entertain them. If the organization is ineffective, the person suffers. There are several ways to analyze an organization. For this discussion I will focus on a few variables that make up organizational effectiveness: philosopy, governance, leadership, cohesiveness, boundary management, routine management, social norms, personnel management, problem resolution, and planning and evaluation. There has been little discussion of organizational variables in human services for severely handicapped individuals. This is surprising. We know from a large body of research on public schools that there are effective and ineffective public schools and that effective ones have several common characteristics (Joyce, Hersh, & McKibbin, 1983). We need to have similar information about community services for severely handicapped people.

The following discussion is based upon our work in setting up group homes, school services, and parent support programs in various communities. Comparative research is sorely needed to verify these ideas. I will briefly discuss a few of these organizational variables; time will not permit a full discussion.

The people who govern and lead the organization share a set of organizing concepts about its purpose and values. Philosophies can be formal or informal, and the two may or may not be the same. In a cohesive organization everyone from the chairperson of the board of directors to the night worker in the group home knows the purpose of her work. Public verbal commitments are translated into behavior and outcomes. In the Project S.A.I.L. homes (Singer & Irvin, 1985) all staff members met weekly with the home director and, at times, with the chairperson of the board of directors; the meetings focused on the indicators of quality of life that the board had decided was important and the tactics or techniques that were effective in meeting goals.

Leadership is a critical variable in effective residential programs. We can create carefully designed service models that will presumably work anywhere. However, unless there is strong leadership even the best service model can fail to deliver a good quality of life. The organization's director needs to be able to work directly with residents as a major portion of his/her job and be able to model technically correct and friendly ways of interaction. He or she also needs to be skilled in other managerial roles; of special importance is staff training and personnel management. The organizational leadership also needs to manage effectively boundaries within the organization and between it and the external environment. For example, a common time in which programming breaks down in group homes is when shifts change; effective leaders establish ways for information to flow across the boundary formed by the shift schedule. Other boundaries include the home's relationship to the neighborhood and the agency's relationship to other community services. If well managed, these relationships bring benefits to the residents; if not, individuals and organizations are placed under stress.

Programmatic leadership and role modeling are made all the more important if residents are individuals who exhibit self-injurious behavior (SIB) or other severe aberrant behaviors. SIB is a complex and often difficult to treat problem. Examples of SIB include head banging, hitting other body parts against objects, biting, slapping, or hitting other body parts, ruminating, vomiting, and eye gouging. These kinds of behavior keep many individuals in highly restrictive environments, often living in various forms of restraints. Treatment is often difficult and people who must care for a self-injurious person experience real distress. When treating these kinds of problems, an effective leader is able to model confidence, a strong sense of caring, and technical precision in working with the person who exhibits SIB.

If skilled and energetic leadership is as critical to successful community programming as I believe it is, then we need to be paying a good deal more attention to recruiting and training young leaders. We will have to make careers in the community service system more attractive and we will need to educate leaders about both administration and direct programming for individual residents.

Staff training matters greatly when serving young people who have complicated service needs, including severe problem behaviors. Ongoing training, along with coaching and monitoring, are the primary ways of maintaining effective and positive social interactions. Effective interactions mean that they teach skills or appropriate behavior. Positive interactions mean that they are friendly and respectful. In our staff training program (Singer, 1986) we have analyzed specific recurring forms of staff/resident interactions. We explain these interaction patterns and show videotapes of them to staff. This idea came from contact with the Achievement Place Model for troubled teenagers (Phillips & Fixen, 1975). In their model, they train houseparents in how to carry out a teaching interaction. These teaching interactions take some different forms when one party is nonverbal. But, in the same way, they can be analyzed and taught. One critical kind of social interaction involves learning to attend to the person's ways of making requests, protesting, and indicating (Riechle & Keogh, 1986). Videotapes of an individual resident's ways of communicating can be used to train staff to identify and respond to idiosyncratic forms of communication.

For the most part, staff of residential programs including foster parents are unskilled people who have had minimal formal training. They must become competent paraprofessionals. People with deaf-blindness and other handicapping conditions are often very complex in the ways that they give and receive communication, in their dietary and medical needs, and their need for structured environments to manage problem behavior. In order to learn and then use many caregiving skills, ongoing staff training needs to be a regular part of the organization. With the high rates of staff turnover in most residential programs there is a constant need for training new staff, for reminding old staff or their mission, and for continually upgrading skills. We believe that the person who has major responsibility for this training ought to be the one who hires and fires other personnel and who leads the organization. Some of the training can be delegated and perhaps some of it can be automated. But the director needs to be seen as an excellent example of how to be a friendly and effective assistant and educator with people who live in the home.

In order to address some of the problems of providing ongoing staff training, my colleagues and I at the Oregon Research Institute have been conducting research and development on the use of microcomputers connected to video recorders as a way to provide important parts of staff training for paraprofessionals. In one study we trained a paraprofessional to utilize four new teaching techniques with a deaf-blind child. Our data show that, in each case, a young paraprofessional was able to implement unfamiliar procedures by using computer-assisted video lessons (Singer, Sowers, & Irvin, in press). We believe that this new technology can be an important tool for staff development with paraprofessionals. Ongoing staff training is one of the most important ways to establish and keep a positive climate or culture within a community service organization. It helps to establish desirable social norms for staff behavior.

The social norms that prevail in an organization are the often unspoken standards that govern an employee's behavior. A difficult set of norms to establish is that a group home or foster home is both a home for the residents and place of work for the people who are paid to provide care. Work norms and domestic norms are usually very different. Well-managed residential programs are careful to make work expectations and standards very clear when they orient and train staff. Effective directors watch for ways that the program may drift away from the desired standards and act to correct them. In addition to a work ethic, another important norm concerns behaviors that indicate respect, such as careful attention to a resident's communicative behavior and preferences. Once again the model of Achievement Place suggested to us that we could deliberately identify and train the kinds of behaviors implied by norms of respect and friendliness. In programs that serve individuals with severe problem behaviors there needs to be a norm that places a lot of value on precision, structure, and planning in interacting with a resident who exhibits aberrant behavior.

Another important organizational variable has to do with providing incentives and ways to elicit commitment from caregivers. Unfortunately, in many programs pay is low and the work is very demanding. As a result, employee turnover rates in community programs are often very high. Lakin reported annual rates of turnover averaging 80% in his survey of residential programs (1981). These problems can be compounded when the program serves individuals with severe problem behaviors. In studies of job stress for special educators and residential care providers, dealing with aberrant behaviors is usually one of th highest rated items since severe aberrant behaviors are highly aversive to most people. In working with dangerous behavior or even life-threatening behavior, staff often are working under conditions similar to those in a hospital emergency room. Staff have to be highly trained and they have to be able to control their own actions to behave in very precise and consistent ways. This is a tall order for someone who has had little formal training and is minimally paid. Effective organizations work hard to keep good people by offering recognition, a sense of group purpose, job advancement, and opportunities to make unique contributions to the program. Effective organizations can make efforts to reduce the effects of stress and to build nonmonetary job incentives but organizations also are strongly influenced by the broader context in which they exist.

Community Services

Community services are extremely important contributors to the quality of life of people in community living arrangements. I will briefly mention three of these: (a) the availability of generic services such as medical, dental, and dietician services; (b) the quality of case management services; and (c) personalized and effective guardianship and advocacy program. All are vital to deinstitutionalization. Placement in the community does not automatically ensure that needed, related services will be available. For example, recent reports express concern about the quality of medical and pharmacological monitoring of mentally retarded persons living in the community (Garrard, 1983). In working with individuals who exhibit aggression or self-injurious behavior, it is important to have medical consultation. Other service agencies such as the local police and the staff at the emergency room of the local hospital may have a role. Often these people have had no prior experience with severely handicapped individuals and our behavioral and educational approaches may be quite foreign to them.

A crucial player in obtaining these and other services can be a case manager. When case managers are knowledgeable about the people whom they serve, have manageable case loads, and work for well-managed organizations, they can be of tremendous benefit to individual service recipients (Magreb & Elder, 1980). A service that has been very impressive in our work with families of children who are deaf-blind and have other severe handicaps is a direction service. Direction services specialize in connecting people and their families who experience disabilities to generic services (Zeller, 1980). They use a case manager model. In our family support research at the Oregon Research Institute we have found direction service to be valued highly by parents and service providers alike (Singer & Irvin, 1985).

Personalized guardianship and advocacy services hold enormous potential for maintaining quality services. Someone who knows an individual resident well and who is a good friend to him or her over a long period of time needs to have whistle-blowing authority. We have to find ways to create and maintain strong personal commitments that endure for the individuals whom we serve. Many parents play this role. But many persons who are deaf-blind have little family contact and no one lives forever. Some of the innovations developed by Apolloni and his colleagues (Apolloni & Cooke, 1984) hold great promise in this respect.

Another level of the service system consists of national and regional philosophies, policies, and funding. Briefly the philosophy of service provision has a powerful directive influence on all levels of the system. The concepts of normalization, equal access, and the developmental model shape much of our efforts. Our present philosophies are challenged and sometimes stretched to the limit in serving individuals who exhibit very severe problem behavior. Our desire to give access to integrated, normal, and friendly community settings can conflict with the need to provide treatment and safety for persons with severe handicaps and the people who work with them.

On the levels of philosophy and policy, there is now a heated debate about what kinds of behavioral treatments are acceptable in the community. TASH and the executive committee of ARC have come out with policies against the use of most kinds of aversive procedures. These policies have, in part, been in response to the apparent misuse and abuse of some behavior modification techniques. Often underfunded programs with untrained staff have relied on poorly designed and brutal procedures to control people with violent behavior in barren environments. TASH has contributed to a much needed movement to encourage the development of nonaversive treatment procedures. I believe however that we make an error if we ban outright all aversive procedures in community programs. In some cases, they may be the only effective alternative to nontreatment. These cases are few and far between. The great majority of individuals with severe problem behaviors, I believe, will respond to carefully structured positive environments and well-designed decelerative programs based upon detailed antecedent analysis and positive reinforcement of adaptive behaviors. However, for some individuals—notably, those who have long established histories of extreme aberrant behavior--these procedures alone may not work, and banning of some aversive alternatives may consititute a failure to provide needed treatment. In our work we have addressed this issue by establishing local human rights review committees and prima facie rules against the use of aversive or restrictive practices (Irvin & Singer, 1985). We believe that this policy alternative along with other necessary components of a comprehensive community service system can provide a vehicle for ensuring that individuals receive treatment while protecting them from inappropriate treatment. This issue deserves a much longer discussion but I believe it is an important example of how attempts to serve individuals with severe aberrant behaviors affects the top levels of the service system. They challenge us to examine and specify how our philosophical commitments apply in morally complex circumstances.

State and National

Another level of the system that ultimately shapes the quality of life of severely handicapped persons is that of federal and state legislation. Laws and regulations establish the parameters of many services. Recent efforts to reform Title XIX are familiar. Reform of Medicaid could help to dismantle the costly and failed system of institutions and to provide much needed fiscal support to community programming (Fernald, 1986). Although a shared mission and ideology can have an amazing power to mobilize people, money is also essential.

Federal funding for all programs for developmentally disabled persons represents less than 1% of the federal budget and less than two tenths of one percent of the GNP (Braddock, 1986). Even a brief glance at our current national defense budget might make us wonder about society's priorities. Those of us who believe in community services for everyone must be careful that their ideals are not used by legislators who are motivated primarily by the desire to cut costs. We should remember that many of the homeless, mentally ill people who now populate our streets are the victims of another deinstitutionalization movement.

Community residential services may be more efficient and cost effective than institutional care. However, at present, Title XIX waiver funding of community alternatives to the institution, in many cases, represents comparatively drastic cuts in community service funding compared to the institutional services that are being replaced.

Certainly we can save money—perhaps 10-20%—but we pay a terrible cost in quality of services when, for example, the going rate for institutional care is $120 a day and the highest possible reimbursement rate in the community is $60. These severe differentials in commitment of resources will not work when it comes to serving many of the most severely handicapped people who now make up the majority of the residual population in institutions.

While people who have needs for intensive behavioral interventions can be served effectively in the community, the services are relatively expensive. In order to employ people who can lead community organizations in the way I described earlier, we have to pay attractive salaries. In order to provide the high staff to resident ratios that are needed to deliver nonaversive behavior management programs, we need to be able to hire large numbers of staff. In order to provide working conditions that will attract and keep good direct service staff, we have to be able to provide a decent base rate of pay, vacations, benefits, and time for job development. Drastic reductions in funding as a person is placed in community services are not wise measures for individuals with needs for intensive behavioral services.

Individuals with extreme problem behaviors do pose a real challenge to the community service system. It has been met in many model programs. Donellan, LaVigna, Zambito, and Thvedt (1985) have reported on successful intensive in-home services for individuals with severe problem behaviors. McGee (1986) has reported on services in Nebraska that emphasize staff-intensive, highly concentrated behavioral interventions that use nonaversive procedures. My colleagues and I have reported on group home programs that have successfully served very challenging young people in California (Singer, Close, Irvin, Gersten, & Sailor, 1984). Smith (1985) described intensive treatment of severe problem behaviors of autistic adults in community home and work settings in Rhode Island. These and similar efforts need to be extended so that we can offer a high quality of life to all people who experience severely handicapping conditions.

Research and demonstration efforts are needed in the following related areas: organizational variables associated with good living environments, nonaversive treatment of severe problem behaviors, staff development and training technologies and procedures, early screening and treatment of aberrant behavior, effective guardianship and advocacy services, early support to families to prevent institutionalization and out-of-home placement, ways to promote and maintain social support to persons residing in group homes, and ways to assess the quality of social interactions and individual affect.

References

Apolloni, T., & Cooke, T. P. (1984). A new look at guardianship. Baltimore: Brookes Publishing.

Apolloni, T., Cappuccilli, J., & Cooke, T. P. (Eds.). (1980). Achievements in residential services for persons with disabilities. Baltimore: University Park Press.

Bercovici, S. (1981). Qualitative methods and cultural perspectives in the study of deinstitutionalization. In R. H. Bruininks, C. E. Meyers, B. B. Sigford, & K. C. Lakin (Eds.). Deinstitutionalization and adjustment of mentally retarded people. (Monograph 4). Washington, D.C.: American Association on Mental Deficiency.

Bogdan, R., Taylor, S., Grandpre, B. D., & Haynes, S. (1977). Attendants' perspectives and programmin on wards in state schools. In B. Blatt, D. Biklen, & R. Boydan (Eds.), An alternative textbook in special education (pp. 85-104). Denver: Love Publishing.

Braddock, D. (1986). Direct cost of institutional care in the United States. Mental Retardation, 24(1), 9-17.

Close, D. W. (1977). Community living for severely and profoundly retarded adults: A group home study. Education and Training of the Mentally Retarded, 12, 256-262.

Cohen, S., & Syme, S. L. (Eds.). (1985). Social support and health. Orlando: Academic Press.

Conroy, J., Efthimiou, J., & Lemanowicz, J. (1982). A matched comparison of the developmental growth of institutionalized and deinstitutionalized mentally retarded clients. American Journal of Mental Deficiency, 86(6), 581-587.

Curtis, W. S., & Donlon, E. T. (1984). A ten year follow-up study of deaf-blind children. Exceptional Children, 50(5), 449-454.

Donellan, A. M., LaVigna, G. W., Zambito, J., & Thvedt, J. (19). A time limited intensive intervention program model to support community placement for persons with severe behavior problems. The Journal of the Association for Persons with Severe Handicaps, 10(3), 123-131.

Elder, J. O., & Magrab, P. R. (1980). Coordinating services to handicapped children. Baltimore: Brookes Publishing.

Gage, M. A., Fredericks, H. D., Baldwin, V., Moore, W., & Grove, D. (1978). Group homes for handicapped children. In N. G. Haring & D. D. Bricker (Eds.), Teaching the severely handicapped (pp. 263-281). Columbus, Ohio: Special Press.

Garrard, S. D. (1983). Community health issues. In J. L. Matson, & J. A. Mulick (Eds.), Handbook of Mental Retardation. New York: Pergammon Press.

Gates, C. F. (1985). Survey of multiply handicapped visually impaired children in the Rocky Mountain/Great Plains region. Journal of Visual Impairment and Blindness, 79(9), 385-390.

Halpern, A., Close, D., & Walker, D. (1985). On my own. Baltimore: Brookes Publishing.

Hill, B. K., Lakin, K. C., & Bruinincks, R. H. (1984). Trends in residential services for people who are mentally retarded: 1977-1982. Journal of the Association for Persons with Severe Handicaps, 9(4), 243-250.

Hitzing, W. (1980). Encor, & Beyond. In T. Apolloni, J. Cappuccillini, & ?. Cooke (Eds.), Achievements in residential services for persons with disbilities. Baltimore: University Park Press.

Irvin, L, & Singer, G. H. (1985). Human rights committee in public schools. Unpublished manuscript, Oregon Research Institute. Eugene, OR.

Jacobson, J. W., & Janicki, M. P. (1985). Functional and health status characteristics of persons with severe handicaps in New York State. Journal of the Association for Persons with Severe Handicaps, 10(1), 51-60.

Joyce, B. R., Hersh, R. H., & McKibbin, M. (1983). The structure of school improvement. New York: Longman, Inc.

Lakin, K. C., Hill, B. K., Hauber, F. A., & Bruinicks, R. H. (1983). New admissions and readmissions to a national sample of public residential facilities. American Journal of Mental Deficiency, 88, 13-20.

LaVigna, G. W., & Donnellan, A. M. (1986). Alternatives to punishment. New York: Irvington.

Magreb, P. R., & Elder, J. O. (Eds.). (1980). Coordinating services to handicapped children. Baltimore: Paul Brookes.

Phillips, _., & Fixen, _., (1975). Residential treatment for troubled children: _____ service delivery systems. In _____, G. T. Bellamy, & B. Wilcox (Eds.), Human _____ at work. Baltimore: Paul Brookes.

Riechle, J., & Keogh, W. J. (1986). Communication instruction for learners with severe handicaps: Some unresolved issues. In R. H. Horner, L. H. Meyer, & H. D. Fredericks (Eds.), Education of learners with severe handicaps. Baltimore: Paul Brookes.

Romer, L. (1986). Lifestyles of severely handicapped individuals in community residences. In this volume.

Scheerenberger, R. C. (1981). Deinstitutionalization: Trends and difficulties. In R. H. Bruininks, C. E. Meyers, B. B. Sigford, & K. C. Lakin (eds.), Deinstitutionalization and adjustment of mentally retarded people. (Monograph Number 4). Washington, D.C.: The American Association of Mental Deficiency.

Singer, G. H., & Irvin, L. (1985). The support and education for families model. Unpublished manuscript, Oregon Research Institute. Eugene, OR.

Singer, G., Sowers, J., & Irvin, L. (1986). Computer assisted video instruction for training paraprofessionals in rural special education programs. Journal of Special Education Technology 8(1), 27-34.

Singer, G. H. S. (1986). Community Living: A training home manual. Portland, OR: Ednic Publishing.

Singer, G. H. S., Close, D. W., Irvin, L. K., Gersten, R., & Sailor, W. (1984). An alternative to the institution for young people with severely handicapping conditions in a rural community. Journal of the Association for Persons with Severe Handicaps, 9(4), 251-261.

Smith, M. D. (1985). Managing the aggressive and self-injurious behavior of adults disabled by autism. Journal of the Association for Persons with Severe Handicaps, 10(4), 228-232.

Taylor, S. J., McCord, W., & Searl, S. J. (1981). Medicaid dollars and community homes: The community ICF/MR controversy. Journal of the Association for the Severely Handicapped, 6(3), 59-64.

Wolf, E. G., Delk, M. T., & Schein, J. D. (1982). Needs assessment of services to deaf-blind individuals. Unpublished manuscript, U.S. Department of Education contract #300-31-0425.

Wolfensberger, W., & Glenn, L. (1975). Pass 3. A method for the quantitative evaluation of human services (Handbook, 3rd ed.). Toronto: National Institute on Mental Retardation.

Zeller, R. W. (1980). Direction service: Collaboration one case at a time. In J. O. Elder & P. R. Magrab (Eds.), Coordinating services to handicapped children. Baltimore: Brookes Publishing.

In Response to Lyle T. Romer

Trends and Issues in Developing Community Living Programs
for Young Adults Who Are Deaf-Blind and Profoundly Handicapped

Stephen S. Barrett

Introduction

Lyle Romer's excellent paper on quality assurance in community living programs for those who are multiply handicapped with deafness and blindness explores the apparent strengths and weaknesses of current approaches while proposing a model that deals objectively with what, by nature, must lend itself to subjective measure. Dr. George Singer, in his response, comes to terms with that challenging issue in light of the frequent inability of these people to communicate personalized feelings of satisfaction.

The goals of my contribution are to (a) present trends and issues observed in community living programs for people who are deaf-blind; (b) identify the population of concern and present its definition according to various sources; (c) present a functional description based upon observation; (d) focus upon a continuum of community living alternatives; and (e) consider the role of parents in planning, funding, and implementation of new programs. Several issues which are inherent in increasing the availability of community living options for people who are deaf-blind and profoundly handicapped will be discussed.

Defining the Population

Most efforts to define "deaf-blindness" have been concerned with eligibility for service, while attempting to reflect how the condition affects ability to function in different domains.

The U. S. Department of Education's Office of Special Education Programs (SEP) defines deaf-blind children as those who have "concomitant hearing and visual impairments, the combination of which causes such severe communication and other developmental and educational problems that they cannot be accommodated in special education programs solely for deaf or blind children" (Federal Register, 1977, p. 42,479).

Rehabilitation Services Administration (RSA), also administered under the Department of Education, defines a deaf-blind person as one who is considered legally blind under the laws relating to vocational rehabilitation in their state, and "who has a chronic hearing impairment so severe that most speech cannot be understood with optimum amplification and the combination of the two disabilities causes extreme difficulty for the person to attain independence in activities of daily living, psychosocial adjustment, or in the pursuit of a vocational objective" (Konar & Rice, 1984, p. 14).

In spite of the widely publicized number of children born with deaf-blindness during the rubella epidemic of 1963-65, the incidence of deaf-blindness among children in America has been stable. Statistics provided by State Coordinators for Deaf-Blind Children, working in programs funded under Title VI-C of the Education of the Handicapped Act as amended, and administered on the federal level by Special Education Programs, report a steady incidence of the condition (SEP, 1985).

Statistics presented by age groupings in 1974 (Dantona, 1974) and eleven years later in 1985 (SEP, 1985) are remarkably similar in disputing the notion that we face only the challenge of serving individuals born during the 1963-65 epidemic (See Table 1).

Table 1.

Summary of Deaf-blind Students by Age Grouping
1974, 1985

Age Group	Dantona (1974)	SEP (1985)
0-2	60	149
3-5	415	436
6-11	2241	920
12-17	852	998
18-21	315	1031
Age unknown	408	736
Total	4,414	4,270

Two observations can be made. First, the "bulge" of students in 1974 was clearly in the 0-11 combined age grouping as compared to 12-21 years in 1985, reflecting the "aging out" of the population. Second, the incidence of deaf-blindness among young children ages 0-11 is higher in 1985 (1,505) than it was in 1974 (1,278). The latter is no doubt at least partially attributable to advancements in identification of children with severe handicapping conditions and the growing sophistication of medical treatment which has enhanced the survival rate of these children.

Obviously, demographics such as these give limited information on the characteristics of the population. A seven-year study of the medical characteristics of 141 children diagnosed as deaf-blind, conducted by the Siegel Institute for Communicative Disorders at Michael Reese Hospital in Chicago, reported high incidences of neurological disorders, orthopedic problems, language and communication disorders, and other medical problems present in addition to vision and hearing impairment (Stein, Palmer, & Weinberg, 1980).

More recent research has focused on the delayed manifestations of the Congential Rubella Syndrome, including diabetes, thyroid disease, ocular damage and other effects (Sever, South, & Shaver, 1985), and the impact upon family dynamics (Appell, 1985).

Population of Concern

The greatest portion of youth born with deaf-blindness during the rubella epidemic of 1963-65 now falls in the age range of 21 to 23 years. As they leave Special Education services which are mandated through age 21 in most states, parents, educators, and posteducation service providers must consider those gains which have been made and what service options are needed to meet the future needs of this population.

Fullest participation in the least restrictive community-based environment, with the individual allowed to make the most of self-help and independent living skills acquired through Special Education programming, is the ideal. Neither custodial care in large institutions nor total dependence upon family members throughout adulthood is a humane or cost effective option.

Even with support services available for those parents who choose to have their children live at home, many parents are not able or willing for this to occur. Having a young adult who is severely handicapped live at home with parents or other family members should always be an option or choice that is available, but it should never become the only alternative to institutionalization.

The author once had the privilege of presenting testimony before the Texas Legislature's Senate Committee on Human Resources in support of Senate Bill 320 which subsequently authorized funds to establish two model Community Living Programs for young adults who are deaf-blind and multihandicapped. A descriptive narrative of the population, based upon many years of direct contact and observation, concluded that

> many of these children . . . have additional handicapping conditions including congenital heart defects, orthopedic problems, cleft palate, and (whether correctly or not) have been diagnosed as being mentally retarded. The children survived, and for the past dozen years, have been served in special education programs designed and funded to meet their needs.
>
> They have been striving to master the most basic of self-help skills, including communication, dressing, feeding and travel. Most of these kids have a long ways to go, and unfortunately, some will never completely master these tasks which the rest of us take for granted. Many will need continued training and supervised living services (Barrett, 1981, p. 5).

While not particularly eloquent, the description is probably still valid today. The primary difference, of course, is that "children" have now become young adults.

Some Hard Questions

In considering the planning and development of Community Living Programs (CLPs) for young adults who are deaf-blind and/or profoundly handicapped, there are several issues of a philosophical nature that must be explored, as direction and focus of plan development are often determined by philosophical values. I refer to these as "hard questions" for obvious reasons and because no two people will necessarily agree on their resolution.

Issue 1. What Constitutes Deinstitutionalization?

Deinstitutionalization of persons with severe handicaps is a topic of great importance, with philosophical, economic, and legalistic ramifications. The term itself can be used to describe the systematic movement of persons with severe handicaps from large, segregated facilities into smaller community-based programs. It can also describe a process which entails the social, economic, and bureaucratic issues pertaining to reallocation of funds from institutional to community settings (Lakin & Bruininks, 1985).

Issue 2. Deinstitutionalization vs. Depopulation

In some states the emphasis is on the latter, with many individuals with severe disabilities being placed in nursing homes or other living arrangements which provide total custodial care. The two concepts must not be confused. One gives hope for movement to a less restrictive community-based environment with an atmosphere conductive to personal growth and community integration; the other gives up virtually all hope.

It is not uncommon these days to hear that a certain state has plans to reduce the size of its institutionalized population from perhaps 2,600 persons to 300 individuals. We should never hesitate to question the quality of life afforded those 300 individuals still institutionalized and to advocate their community placement. Appropriate planning and resources must be applied to make certain that individuals with the severest disabilities, including young adults who are deaf-blind and multiply handicapped, are not overlooked.

Issue 3. Reinstitutionalization

There must be concern for the many youth served under P.L. 94-142 and educated in public school settings who are exiting the school systems in large numbers. Without appropriate planning and development of Community Living Alternatives, many young adults who are deaf-blind are not going to be able to live in the community and will ultimately be placed back in institutional settings.

Issue 4. Personal Value Systems

Do you believe the goal of transition to be a smooth continuum and expansion of services from the arena of education to life in the community, with the individual afforded the opportunity to live as naturally and fully independently as possible? What level of importance should be placed upon the belief system of an agency or individual? People who are deaf-blind or profoundly handicapped and in transition from Special Education to post-education services, their families and advocates, have the right to know the value systems of agencies charged with the responsibility of providing services. These rights are expressed in Table 2 (Barrett, 1986).

Issue 5. Transition as Criteria of Success

Transition to community-based services, including options for employment, leisure, and recreation (all provided in a natural community environment) should not only be the goal of Special Education but also the final criterion of its success. How else can the investment of tens of millions of dollars devoted to special education of children and youth with deaf-blindness be justified?

The Range of Community Living Options

Programs attempting to develop community living services must consider the needs of the individuals to be served, their anticipated needs of supervision in community-based residences, and the range of appropriate models. As pointed out by Dr. Singer in this publication, the population of individuals who are deaf-blind is as diverse and

Table 2

**Declaration of Rights of Young Adults with Disabilities
in Transition to Community-based Services**

The philosophical foundations of transition have several components which set forth its goals and purpose. These include the following:

1. People with disabilities have the right to live in the community, in regular integrated neighborhoods, and have access to all the community has to offer.

2. They have the right to meaningful employment, working with nondisabled co-workers in regular employment, earning fair wages, with whatever support and supervision is necessary for them to become successful.

3. The above services, including opportunities for leisure and recreation, must be provided in natural community environments that encourage interaction with other members of the community.

---

heterogeneous as any population of individuals with disabilities. No one model or degree of supervision will meet the needs of more than a few individuals.

Table 3 represents a continuum of community living options based upon degree of supervision provided, ranging from heavily supervised to minimal or no supervision (Lessard, 1984). A broad range of options, with narrative description of each is presented in Table 4, ranging from least restrictive to most restrictive (Cotten, in press).

Table 3

**A Continuum of Supervised and Semi-independent Living Options
in the Community (Lessard, 1984, p.16)**

Intermediate Care Facility (ICF-MR) --------------------	Heavily Supervised
Community Residence Programs -------------------------	Moderately Supervised
Staffed Apartments ----------------------------------	Live-in Staff Supervisor
Semisupervised Apartment Living ---------------------	Support Staff Only
Independent Living ----------------------------------	No Scheduled Support

---

Parent Involvement in Planning, Funding, Implementation

In a later section, I will present trends observed while visiting and participating in the development of Community Living Programs (CLPs) for young adults who are deaf-blind. However, one trend is particularly noteworthy and commendable, and that is the high degree of parent involvement in all phases of planning, funding, and implementation of CLPs in five states.

Table 4. Alternative Living Arrangements (ALA)
(Cotten, in press)

1. OWN HOME -- This is a place where the person lives as a responsible member of a family, or alone, with at least half of the responsibility for the operation of the home.

2. APARTMENT -- This is an apartment where the person lives, again assuming at least half of the responsibility for the operation of the apartment.

3. SHADOW SUPERVISION -- This is an ALA where the individual lives in an apartment and receives only minimal supervision and training from a person living within close proximity.

4. SHARE-A-HOME -- The individuals are able to care for their own personal needs but, for a variety of reasons, are unable to live alone. This is a complementary arrangement where each member contributes to the overall operation of the homes.

5. SUPERVISED APARTMENT -- This is an ALA which enables a person to live in an apartment setting with supervision and habilitative training from individuals living within the same apartment complex.

6. GROUP HOME -- This is a home providing supervision and training in a home environment with live-in house parents. Individuals should have basic self-help skills, a means of communication, the ability and motivation to go to a day program, and should demonstrate a level of social skills which is acceptable in the community.

7. PERSONAL CARE HOME -- This is an establishment operated and maintained to provide residential accommodations, personal services, and social care to individuals who are not related to the licensee and who, because of impaired capacity for self-care, elect or require protective living accommodations but do not have an illness, injury, or disability for which regular medical care and 24-hour nursing service is required.

8. FOSTER HOME -- A foster home is the home of a person or family group not related to the client who cares for one person or more on a free basis.

9. ICF/MENTAL RETARDATION -- A facility for mentally retarded persons, established primarily for the diagnosis, treatment, and habilitation of the individual. It provides 24-hour supervised residential living with individualized habilitation services geared to help each resident reach and maintain his maximum functioning capabilities.

10. INTERMEDIATE CARE FACILITY -- A health-related institution planned, organized, operated and maintained to provide facilities and services (which are supportive, restorative, and preventive in nature, with related social care), to individuals who, because of a physical or mental condition, or both, require care in an institutional environment but do not have an illness, injury, or disability for which regular medical care and 24-hour nursing services are required.

11. ICF/SNF -- A transition from ICF to SNF for those individuals who are becoming medically frail.

12. SKILLED NURSING FACILITY -- A health-care institution planned, organized, operated and maintained to provide facilities and health services with related social care to inpatients who require medical care and 24-hour nursing services for illness or disability.

This involvement is perhaps most evident in Texas, New Jersey, Illinois, Florida, and South Carolina, among others. That is to say, the development of CLPs in these states would not have occurred without the leadership and driving force of the parents.

In Texas, members of the parent organization met with service providers to form an Interagency Task Force on Future Services to Deaf-Blind Persons. This has now been in existence for seven years. An initial goal was to formulate a legislative package requesting state authorization and appropriations to conduct statewide identification and needs assessment of Texans, who were deaf-blind, and to establish up to three CLP models across the state.

After considerable effort, primarily on the part of the parents, these services and programs were implemented. Parents played the lead role in reaching out to service providers, contacting local legislators, coordinating advocacy for CLPs and the bills introduced before the legislature. They played major role in implementation and have a continuing role in monitoring quality of service.

The Task Force itself has enjoyed a series of major accomplishments in its short history, including statewide and regional training, support for local interagency efforts, advocacy, public service announcements, service directories, dissemination of information, and the joint development of a Model Transition Plan.

Activities in other states have been no less successful and in each it has been the parents who played the lead role. In New Jersey and Illinois, for example, parents have been extremely successful in working with state and privately funded organizations to secure commitments for initial construction costs, day program alternatives, staff, and other needs. Each has benefited from the support of a strong interagency coalition of parents, family members, and service providers. In Florida and South Carolina, parents have helped launch efforts to plan and implement new community living services based upon interagency cooperation.

In past years, activities such as these developed in isolation with few models being presented and little in the way of technical assistance. However, this is changing rapidly through the efforts of the two SEP-funded Technical Assistance Centers in deaf-blindness, which became operational October 1, 1984.

Newer efforts to establish CLPs, in states such as Florida, South Carolina, and others, don't have to "re-invent the wheel" and can learn from the efforts of others with technical assistance provided by Helen Keller National Center and The Association for Persons with Severe Handicaps (TASH).

At the beginning of our Technical Assistance Center project, we were able to identify thirteen different programs which had established CLPs. We visited many of these programs, met with their staff, and observed a continuum of services ranging from those programs providing minimal assistance and supervision to individuals living in their own apartments to those providing much more intensive support to individuals with multiple medical and self-care needs.

During 1985, our project sponsored three national and bi-regional training workshops on all aspects of developing CLPs, held in Dallas, Washington, and New York. These were attended by representatives of over 100 agencies. Follow-up contact with participants has allowed us to identify ten additional states where agencies are seriously attempting to replicate existing models or to establish new approaches to community living. We are developing intensified technical assistance plans to assist those agencies in their efforts.

Additional Trends in CLPs

Several trends are apparent among those efforts, including the previously mentioned role of parents (see Table 5).

Table 5

**Trends Observed in Developing Community Living Programs for
Young Adults Who Are Deaf-Blind**

---

1. Parents of youth with deaf-blindness are playing the lead roles in almost all of these states. Well-organized parent associations have approached their state legislatures and state agencies for funding and support. In four particular states, there are new community living programs becoming operational almost exclusively due to the work of parent organizations. This important trend is becoming the rule rather than the exception as all ten states we are currently working with have strong parent involvement.

2. Funding sources other than federal dollars are being tapped. Four states have obtained sponsorship and funding through religious organizations and two states are relying almost 100% on state-appropriated dollars. Another source being utilized is that of real estate syndication.

3. Interagency planning of community living programs is occurring. Typically involved are such programs as Special Education, State V.R., Mental Health, Mental Retardation, Developmental Disabilities, Public Health, local service organizations, parents, and consumer organizations.

The Issue of Categorical vs. Integrated Settings

There can be no doubt that many issues remain in developing community living services for young adults who are deaf-blind. Paramount is the issue of what constitutes an integrated setting and the feasibility of including persons who are deaf-blind within either CLPs established for persons with other handicaps or in full integration with nonhandicapped peers.

The Transition Case Manager hoping to facilitate community-based residential placements for young adults who are deaf-blind and/or profoundly handicapped faces a dilemma. Few CLPs providing minimal supervision to clients feel comfortable serving people who are deaf-blind. On the other hand, programs designed specifically for young adults who are deaf-blind are still relatively scarce and may be years from implementation in many states.

There are indeed individuals educated under the category of "deaf-blind" who possess a greater degree of functional use of vision and hearing than others. These are the fortunate ones whose needs may be adequately met in existing programs.

Program models for persons who are considered mentally retarded lean greatly toward the Semi-Independent Living Program (SILP) model where as little as ten hours of supervision per month is provided (Halpern, Close & Nelson, 1986). Such models have great limitations in providing services to persons who are severely or profoundly handicapped (Lakin & Bruininks, 1985). Thus the dilemma.

Service agencies dveloping CLPs exclusively for people who are deaf-blind may have had little choice due to the reluctance of other agencies to include individuals who are deaf-blind for lack of training, qualified staff, or other considerations. Additionally, the population served is often determined by the funding source of the CLP or service mandates which are categorical in nature.

Staff working in Special Education, Vocational Rehabilitation, programs for the Developmentally Disabled, or other service systems attempting to plan and provide transition services for persons who are deaf-blind frequently encounter such obstacles, which are chiefly due to lack of training, awareness, and preparation on the part of local community service providers. All these factors may have contributed to the development of CLPs exclusively for individuals who are deaf-blind.

In spite of how one feels about the complicated questions involved, no one model, regardless of the population it is designed for, can meet the needs of all people (Cotten, in press). It is hoped that people who are deaf-blind can be appropriately served in the full range of community living options described by Lessard (1984) and others, with placement based upon need and in the least restrictive setting.

A Concept of "Supported Living"

Individuals responsible for implementing state-of-the-art vocational programs with persons who are severely or profoundly handicapped have noted the associated need for community living options (Kregel, Wehman & Seyfarth, 1985; Halpern, 1985). Going back 12-13 years, it was the author's experience in conducting competitive job placements of adults with deaf-blindness that obtaining the placement was challenging, yet relatively easy, when compared to attempting to assist the individual in locating suitable housing.

Supported employment theory and practice has several basic components in its structure that appear to be applicable to a model of "Supported Living." These include individualized functional assessment of skills, close supervision—a 1:1 or 1:3 staff-to-worker ratio as indicated, a wide range of employment settings and options, and an approach that says that "whatever support this individual needs on the job site to become a productive worker will be provided" (Barrett, 1986, p. 12).

This unique approach to employment needs to be considered in the process of individualized selection of community living options. The key elements, similar to those observed in supported employment programs, would be in (a) functional assessment of skills in realistic living environments, (b) consideration of the use of residual vision and hearing, if any, (c) specialized use of adaptive equipment or techniques when indicated, (d) close supervision and training, and (e) support provided over an indefinite period of time, as necessary.

There might be similarities to the SILP model reported by Halpern, Close, and Nelson (1986) in the case of individuals who may function well with limited supervision. Differences might be in the areas of staff training, specialized communication skills training, identification and funding of support services, and amount of supervision.

This approach would not be feasible for all persons who are deaf-blind or profoundly handicapped, since there must be a recognition that some have had little or no formal training in self-care skills, have been institutionalized for much, if not all, of their lives, and possess many serious behavior patterns of self-abuse aquired through years of neglect and lack of appropriate service.

However, an approach based totally upon individualized assessment of the person's skills and needs, along with supportive training in actual living environments, could focus on helping each individual live in the least restrictive setting possible.

A concept such as "Supported Living" must become a part of the transition planner's repertoire and should be applied to the greatest extent possible in order to assist young adults who are deaf-blind and profoundly handicapped in reaching their fullest potential for community living.

Conclusions

In reviewing the history of residential placements of young adults who are deaf-blind and/or profoundly handicapped, we find that a few options have traditionally been made available. These have been (a) living at home with parents, siblings, or other relatives, (b) institutionalization, or (c) living in the community in a supportive setting with only as much supervision as was necessary. The first alternative is not always available or desirable and, often in the past, has led to the second one, which is neither humane nor therapeutic. Clearly, it is the third alternative that is caring, humane, cost effective, and achievable.

Organizations hoping to establish community-based living alternatives face tremendous challenges in cost, program design, personnel, and the uncertainty of continued state and federal support. Yet, if transition to community-based services is the goal and final product of Special Education, community living is the key. Parents, service agencies, and advocates must work together to expand the options currently available for community living and to seek new answers to some very hard questions.

References

Appell, M. (1985). The multihandicapped child with congenital rubella: Impact on family and community. Reviews of Infectious Diseases, 7, Suppl. 1.

Barrett, S. (1981, March 2). Testimony on behalf of Senate Bill 320, Senate Committee on Human Resources, Austin, TX.

Barrett, S. (1986, June 7). A national perspective on transition, community living and supported employmnt. Presentation to New Jersey Association of th Deaf-blind, Edison, NJ.

Cotten, P. (in press). Selecting, as a living arrangement, the most appropriate placement for the person who is deaf-blind. In Barrett et al. (Eds.), Vocational Preparation and training of young adults who are deaf-blind.

Dantona, R. (1974). Demographic data and status of services for deaf-blind children in the United States. In C. Sherrick (Ed.), 1980 is now: A conference on the future of deaf-blind children, Los Angeles: John Tracy Clinc.

Federal Register. (1985, October 9). 50(196).

Halpern, A. (1985). Transition: A look at the foundations. Exceptional Children, 51(6), 479-486.

Konar, V., & Rice, D. (1984). Strategies for serving deaf-blind clients. Paper presented at Eleventh Institute on Rehabilitation Issues, Hot Springs: University of Arkansas.

Kregel, J., Wehman, P., & Seyfarth, J. (1985). Community integration of young adults with mental retardation: Transition from school to adulthood. In P. Wehman & J. Hill (Eds.), Competitive employment for persons with mental retardation. Richmond: Virginia Commonwealth University.

Lakin, C., & Bruininks, R. (1985). Strategis for achieving community integration of developmentally disabled citizens. Baltimore: Paul H. Brookes.

Lessard, K. (1984). Transitional services, training programs, and the realities of dcvcloping community-based services for multihandicapped blind and deaf-blind adults. Paper prepared for the American Foundation for the Blind, New York.

Sever, J., South, M., & Shaver, K. (1985). Delayed manifestations of congenital rubella. Reviews of Infectious Diseases, 7(Suppl) 1.

Special Education Programs, U. S. Department of Education, Annual Deaf-blind Student Count Data, 1985.

Stein, L., Palmer, P., & Weinberg, B. (1980). Characteristics of a young deaf-blind population, The Siegel Report, David T. Siegel Institut for Communicativ Disorders, Chicago, IL.

Report of the Working Group on Community-based Housing Options

Group Members

Stephen S. Barrett   David Goode
Stephanie Campo   Jane Polcaro
Michael Collins   Lyle T. Romer
Anne Devereux   George H. S. Singer
Charles Freeman

Report prepared by George H. S. Singer

Introduction

The group met to develop recommendations to policy makers regarding community residential options for young adults who are deaf-blind. The group agreed on the following philosophical premises:

All individuals should have access to the benefits of our society including those people who are the most severely handicapped. The concept of zero exclusion which has been applied to school services should also apply to the provision of community residential services. In developing the following recommendations, the committee focused its concern on the population of individuals who experience severe and multiple handicaps of deaf-blindness. While all severely handicapped persons are deserving of high quality community residential services, our focus was on those persons who are graduating from public school services without having developed complex symbolic communication skills and who may have lifelong need for several services, such as physical therapy, occupational therapy, medical support, behavioral programming, along with assistance with

51

normal activities of daily living. In this context, we did not primarily address the residential needs of those individuals who experience normal intellectual functioning, or those persons with mild to moderate handicaps who possess complex symbolic communication skills and the skills to live in semi-independent settings.

Those individuals, who are profoundly handicapped, who are the focus of our concern, will need intensive lifelong assistance to participate in activities of normal community life. These individuals have, with some rare exceptions, been excluded from community living even in those states which have developed community living options for moderately and severely handicapped individuals. It is our intention to call attention to their needs and to assert that they, too, deserve one of the primary benefits of participation in society—a home. Thus, we assume that all individuals, regardless of the severity of their handicapping conditions, may benefit from small homelike residential living provided that individualized needs for services are fully met.

Public policy is an expression of values; and, as such, we believe that public policy on community-based housing options should reflect the following:

1. Individuals who are deaf-blind should have access to the benefits of our society, including a home in the broadest sense of a place of refuge, individual recognition, and support.
2. Individuals who are deaf-blind should have access to valued daily activities, including work, commerce, and recreation with individuals who are caring, respectful, and who can communicate with them.
3. Individuals who are deaf-blind should have their individual health, communication, and behavioral treatment and training needs met, including the opportunity as adults for continued learning.

Program Characteristics

Programs designed to provide community-based housing options for this population should include the following:

1. Living arrangements that meet the individualized needs of this population including services for communication, mobility, self-care, and physical and mental health needs.
2. Individual case management and advocacy, including individualized needs assessment, service linkage, and monitoring of service delivery. These case management services would make generic community services available.
3. A full array of services to these persons living in natural and foster homes, including transportation, in-home respite, benefits, maintenance, care-giver training, counseling, and adaptive equipment.
4. Quality assurance mechanisms that give a significant voice to parents and related service providers. These mechanisms would prevent abuse and help to maintain valued lifestyles.
5. A system to attract, train, and support high-quality leadership and direct service personnel in the field of residential services.
6. A system and incentives to enlist the personnel development resources of universities, junior colleges, and vocational training programs including innovative programs such as mentorship and apprenticeship.
7. Systems for job advancement and other incentives in order to maintain high quality personnel.

Issues

At present there are severe deficits in public policy and service delivery. These deficits prevail at virtually every level and negatively affect every aspect of the residential service system. In order to ensure quality community-based housing options for those who are profoundly multiply handicapped with deaf-blindness, some of the issues and obstacles which must be addressed include the following:

1. Low public and professional awareness, understanding, and expectations for this population, with a lack of organized advocacy efforts for this low-incidence population.
2. A history of reliance for services for this population on traditional congregate programs that dilute family/community bonds, and the exclusion of this population from new community-based services and programs.
3. A lack of mandated adult services and no single, clearly identified system or agency responsible to provide services.
4. Lack of interagency planning/coordination for services.
5. Lack of commitment to full, long-term funding for quality residential services, and a lack of fiscal commitment to family support services.
6. A lack of alternative incentive mechanisms including communication between business/private industry and social services.
7. The need for a system of adequate compensation and incentives that will attract service personnel who are knowledgeable about sensory deficits and well trained in alternative communication methods and behavior management.
8. A lack of higher education commitment and a lack of federal incentives to prepare service personnel for low-incidence populations, including community service workers, as well as teachers.

Recommendations

1. Individuals who are deaf-blind should be prepared for community living through the following:
   a. Community referenced/intensive school instruction.
   b. Individual Transition Planning (ITP) for students 15 years and over. Each ITP should include, but not be limited to vocational, health, communication, residential, financial, guardianship, and case management concerns.
   c. Training for parents in ways to enhance domestic, community and leisure skills.
2. The development of model demonstration projects for comprehensive family support services should be encouraged and supported.
3. Higher education programs for training leaders in residential services should be created by combining the expertise from teacher training programs with that of other faculties, such as those in business, management, leisure studies, and social work.
4. The technical assistance role of state and multistate centers should be expanded to include training of community service personnel and family members.
5. The use of new technologies to promote staff and family training in community services should be encouraged.
6. Effective dissemination of information about existing quality community services for deaf-blind and other profoundly handicapped individuals should be encouraged and supported.
7. Existing service providers, advocacy, and professional organizations should be informed about the need to serve these and other individuals excluded from community-based options.
8. Information about statewide systems-change efforts from states that have created successful services for these individuals in the community should be disseminated.

9. Planning groups addressing major issues in providing quality services for low incidence populations, e.g., family support services, transition planning, and residential service development, should be convened.
10. The formation of alliances with other advocacy organizations and service providers who serve low-incidence populations should be promoted.

SECTION II. SUPPORTED COMPETITIVE EMPLOYMENT

Supported Competitive Employment for Persons
Labeled Severely and Profoundly Mentally Retarded:
Impact of Wages and Integration

Paul Wehman and Janet W. Hill

Introduction

Within the past several years there has been an intensified interest in helping persons who are challenged with moderate, severe, and profound mental retardation to improve their work opportunities. Specifically, there have been numerous studies and papers which describe successful efforts to establish sheltered enclaves in industry (Mank, Rhodes, & Bellamy, 1986; Rhodes & Valenta, 1985), mobile work crews (Borbeau, 1985), school-based employment activities (Bates & Panscofar, 1983; Brown et al., 1984), and supported competitive employment (Rusch, 1986; Rusch & Mithaug, 1980; Vogelsburg, 1985; Wehman, 1986; Wehman & Hill, 1985; Wehman et al., 1985). This work builds upon earlier work done by leaders in the field such as Bellamy (e.g., Bellamy, Horner, & Inman, 1979) and Gold (1972), whose research focused primarily upon developing work competencies in difficult bench-work manual assembly.

Consistent with these advances in research there have been changes in federal priorities and policy in employment. The Administration on Developmental Disabilities (Elder, 1984) has spearheaded a major initiative regarding employment for persons with disabilities. The Office of Special Education and Rehabilitation Services, U. S. Department of Education, has published key policy papers (Will, 1984) on supported employment as well as sponsored major symposia on costs and benefits associated with employment of persons who are disabled (e. g., February 24, 1986). The Social Security Administration has also funded numerous transitional employment demonstration projects for persons with mental retardation.

While it is clear that during the last three years there has been a powerful movement toward expanding integrated employment opportunities for people labeled severely handicapped, it is equally clear that relatively little published literature has appeared to document the competitive employment success of people with measured intelligence under the level of 40. Competitive employment is defined as work for at least minimum wage in work environments where there are predominantly nonhandicapped workers (Rusch, 1986; Wehman, 1981). Measured intelligence is, of course, not the only indicator of severely handicapping conditions but it can be a powerful means of communicating about a target population. This is especially true when taken in relation to an individual's concomitant behavioral and physical characteristics.

In the Rhodes and Valenta (1985) study, which is a model effort at demonstrating an industry-based enclave, five of eight workers had measured intelligence of over 40. In our work in Virginia only 8% of the entire study population has been reported to have I.Q.s under 40 (Hill, Banks, Hill, Wehman, in press; Wehman et al., 1985). Brown and his colleagues (1984) report nonpaid and paid integrated work opportunities for individuals with severe handicaps. However, with the notable exception of the excellent bench-work models described by Bellamy and his associates (Bellamy et al, 1979; O'Bryan, 1985), which have focused on the most challenged populations, relatively few reports exist which detail the progress and problems of persons who have IQs in the severe and profound range that are actually working or have worked in competitive employment, enclaves, or work crews.

The present article was developed and disseminated through partial support of Grant No. G008301124 from the National Institute of Handicapped Research, and Grant No. G008430106 from Special Education Programs, Secondary and Transition Services.

We are deeply indebted to P. David Banks for his efforts at assembling the data in the tables in this report. We are also grateful to the numerous job coaches who willingly collected the data from which this paper could be developed. Finally, the work and support of Jill White, Carmen Mendez, Connie Britt, Walt Chernish, Judy Sands, Shelia Miller, Lance Elwood and Connie Ford, a local service provider is greatly appreciated.

Paper presented by Paul Wehman.

Therefore, the purpose of this paper is to provide an in-depth look at those individuals labeled as severely or profoundly mentally retarded whom we have helped gain competitive employment over the past eight years. Specifically, we wish to report on their demographic characteristics, nature of employment, financial data, and supervisor evaluation data. It is the intent of this paper to see how these results might have implications for similar vocational interventions with other populations such as those labeled deaf-blind, autistic, and multiply handicapped.

Method

The data presnted in this article were collected by professional service staff who work as industry-based job coaches. Most of the five job coaches either have bachelor's or master's degrees in Special Education, Psychology, Rehabilitation, or Social Work. The data reported in this paper were accumulated throughout the period from 1978-1986. The staff were trained by the authors in data collection and in how to check the accuracy of their data. This competitive employment program took place at a major university in the southeastern part of the United States. The program is characterized as one which focuses exclusively on supported competitive employment (e.g., Rusch, 1986; Wehman & Dregel, 1985; Wehman, 1986).

Briefly, this approach emphasizes vocational intervention directly at the job site after the person is hired. It requires the used of a skilled human services professional who can provide specialized placement and training support. Programs which do not provide this type of ongoing support have consistently been unable to maintain people with serious disabilities in competitive employment.

All data collected have been drawn only from placements of clients for which we had full responsibility. Clients were referred to us from schools, day programs, parents, and rehabilitation counselors. They were drawn from three different geographical locations in the state. Client selection for placement was based on a variety of factors such as parental support, travel accommodations, and job availability. There was less interest or concern about the entering skill level of the person since the supported employment approach was used to overcome whatever client deficits were present.

All client data were stored in a Franklin ACE 1000 computer along with data from many clients with a measured intelligence of over 40. These data are continually updated by a computer programmer and a data entry specialist.

To summarize, clients were referred for services into competitive employment. Those which we could work with had continued levels and amounts of data collected. It is those data which are profiled in this report.

Results

Demographics

The data on 21 persons are described in Table 1. The persons ranged in age from 18 to 63 and in measured intelligence from 24 to 39. The average age of this group was 27, and the average measured intelligence was 31. Four were functionally nonverbal or had severely impaired speech. All were ambulatory. None had independent travel skills prior to placement and about half still lived at home. Only two had the experience of an integrated school, while six had never had any special education. As can be seen from Table 1, a number of persons were replaced into second and third jobs as it became necessary.

Nature of Work

Virtually all individuals worked in entry-level service positions in profit and nonprofit companies (see Table 2). The ratio of handicapped to nonhandicapped persons was usually at least 1:10. Positive work behavior was seen as a major work asset for a

Table 1

Demographic Profile of Individual Workers Labeled Severely and Profoundly Retarded

NAME	AGE	IQ	COMPANY NAME	CLIENT RESIDENCE	START DATE	END DATE	MONTHS WORKED
1	20	39	Howard Johnson's Rest.	Institution	10/31/85	Current	4.11
2	19	24	Chi Chi's Restaurant	Parent	10/24/84	09/09/85	10.51
2	---	---	Morrison's Cafeteria	---	09/16/85	12/18/85	3.06
3	34	25	Community Alternative Inc	Group Home	07/27/83	01/02/85	17.25
4	34	31	Truckstops of America	Superv. Apt.	05/04/84	02/12/85	9.33
5	30	27	University of Richmond	Parent	10/23/78	Current	88.38
6	54	34	General Medical	Group Home	03/02/81	11/01/81	8.02
7	63	36	Medical College of Virginia	Adult Home	02/16/79	Current	84.57
8	36	38	ARA Services	Parent	10/27/80	06/03/81	7.20
8	---	---	ARC Camp Baker	---	06/08/81	07/20/81	1.38
8	---	---	ARA Services	---	08/23/81	Current	54.37
9	37	31	Little Creek Officer Club	Group Home	04/20/81	06/25/82	14.16
9	---	---	Atlantic Cleaners	---	07/07/82	08/05/83	12.94
9	---	---	Colonial Cleaners	---	11/28/83	Current	27.20
10	23	33	Clark's Restaurant	Parent	02/13/83	02/27/83	0.46
10	---	---	Cimmaron Rose	---	05/29/84	06/29/84	1.02
10	---	---	Harry's Lounge	---	08/06/84	02/22/85	6.57
11	23	36	Pancakes-N-Pickles	Parent	03/09/85	08/13/85	5.16
12	24	39	J. C. Penney Company	Parent	01/29/85	Current	13.14
13	26	37	St. Benedictine H. S.	Parent	03/09/81	02/20/84	35.42
14	22	35	Bradlee's #570	Supv. Apt.	09/17/85	Current	5.55
15	22	27	Rustler's Steak House	Parent	11/04/85	02/28/86	3.81
16	19	39	Miller and Rhodes	Parent	12/02/85	Current	3.06
17	21	24	Western Sizzlin / Chester	Parent	10/02/85	Current	5.06
18	25	29	Community Alternative Inc	Parent	01/09/84	Current	25.82
19	36	37	Grace Lutheran Church	Parent	03/30/83	Current	35.19
20	22	38	Western Sizzlin Rest.	Parent	02/19/86	02/28/86	0.30
21	20	32	Plata Grande Restaurant	Parent	01/19/86	Current	1.48

TER - Terminated
RES - Resigned
N/A - Not Appropriate

Nature of Job

NAME	TYPE OF JOB HELD	RATIO OF HANDICAPPED TO NON-HANDICAPPED WORKERS IN INTEGRATED JOB SETTING	GREATEST OBSTACLE	GREATEST ASSET	REASON FOR SEPARATION
1	Food-Dish/pot washer	1/18	---	---	N/A
2	Food-Dish/pot washer	1/15	Continued supervision	Work attitude	RES-Took better job
2	Food-Dish/pot washer	1/15	---	---	TER-Slow work
3	Janitor/Housekeeper	1/15	Low endurance	---	TER-Aberrant behavior
4	Janitor/Housekeeper	1/30	Continued supervision	Likable personality	TER-Required continued prompting
5	Food-Front dining area	2/12	Poor social skills	Likable personality	N/A
6	Assembler/Bench worker	1/8	Aberrant behavior	Work attitude	TER-Poor attendance/ tardiness
7	Food-Back kitchen utility	5/75	Low quality work	Public transportation	N/A
8	Food-Dish/pot washer	2/12	Poor social skills	Attendance/promptness	LO-Seasonal w/return
8	Food-Back kitchen utility	---	Poor social skills	Likable personality	TER-Low quality work
8	Food-Back kitchen utility	2/12	Slow work	Attendance/promptness	N/A
9	Laundry	1/50	---	---	TER-Poor job match
9	Laundry	2/14	Attendance/tardiness	Fast work skills	RES-Transportation problems
9	Laundry	1/10	Transportation	Work attitude	N/A
10	Food-Dish/pot washer	1/20	---	---	RES-Does not want to work
10	Food-Preparation	2/3	Transportation	Work attitude	LO-Economic situation
10	Food-Front dining area	1/3	Interest/Attitude	Parental support	RES-Does not want to work
11	Food-Front dining area	1/8	---	---	RES-Parent initiated
12	Janitor/Housekeeper	1/10	Attendance/Tardiness	Fast work skills	N/A
13	Janitor/Housekeeper	1/10	Low endurance	Fast work skills	RES-Moved away
14	Stock clerk/Warehouse	1/5	---	---	N/A
15	Food-Back kitchen utility	1/5	---	---	LO-economic situation
16	Janitor/Housekeeper	1/20	---	---	N/A
17	Food-Dish/pot washer	1/10	---	---	N/A
18	Janitor/Housekeeper	---	Insub/Aggress/Violent	Attendance/promptness	N/A
19	Janitor/Housekeeper	1/5	Poor appearance	Attendance/promptness	N/A
20	Food-Front dining area	1/10	---	---	TER-Poor attendance/Tardiness

number of the individuals even though most had no previous employment. Slow work speed, poor endurance, and unacceptable work quality were major problems. Not all clients have specific obstacles or assets indicated for them in the table because the evaluating job coaches did not observe any distinguishing characteristics in this area.

Financial Benefits and Costs

Table 3 shows hours worked, wages accumulated, etc. It is notable that none of the persons had ever worked before and had no previous earnings. Most were at home, school, or in adult activity centers. Those who are reported with work levels of less than 20 hours of work per week did so in order to stay in school for longer periods of time. The cumulative earnings of this group were over $200,000 in unsubsidized wages. We also report the average job-coach hours on a monthly basis. This figure was taken over the life of the individual's employment and is reported in order to give a sense of the per placement and maintenance cost involved. A rate of $20 per hour was established for our job coaches' services by the Virginia Department of Rehabilitative Services. Hence, one could multiply the total intervention hours by the $20-per-hour rate and obtain an estimate of costs for each client.

Table 3

Financial Benefits Table

Name	Total Intervention Time Reported in Job Coach Hours	Cumulative Months Worked	Cumulative Wages Earned
1	46:00	4.11	1,260.00
2	485:02	13.57	2,581.36
3	185:35	17.25	9,506.25
4	225:13	9.33	5,494.00
5	1057:03	88.38	31,964.00
6	0:00	8.02	4,103.75
7	617:58	84.57	47,432.88
8	383:44	62.95	31,542.90
9	358:45	54.31	25,182.15
10	222:04	8.05	2,504.60
11	56:55	5.16	462.30
12	151:35	13.14	4,166.00
13	49:51	35.42	19,604.20
14	101:45	5.55	1,340.00
15	304:45	3.81	603.50
16	84:05	3.06	966.00
17	146:15	5.06	1,513.05
18	27:17	25.82	6,925.88
19	262:23	35.19	10,251.00
20	37:10	0.30	161.00
21	53:45	1.48	504.00
	4867:10	484.50	208,068.82

Supervisor Evaluation

Regular supervisor evaluations were also collected in order to determine the individual client's performance according to the company. A number "5" indicated excellent performance with no room for improvement, with a number "1" indicating poor, and a "3" adequate. As Table 4 indicates, most of the individuals in this report were rated as adequate or better after a month or so of work. Interestingly, however, the performance, on-task behavior, and client appearance evaluations decreased over time in the job.

Table 4

Supervisors' Evaluations of Workers with Severe and Profound Handicaps
Evaluation Item

Evaluation Item	Mean/Time	
	Initial Eval.	Latest Eval.
Arrives and leaves on time	4.36842	4.70588
Maintains good attendance	4.57895	4.72222
Takes appropriate meals and breaks	4.50000	4.61111
Maintains good appearance	4.22222	4.05556
Performance comparable to others	4.00000	3.87500
Communication not a problem	3.68421	3.77778
Consistent attention to job tasks	4.21053	3.88889
Overall appraisal of proficiency	3.16667	3.27778

Discussion

The data described in this paper present simultaneously a positive and a negative view of competitive employment prospects for people labeled severely and profoundly retarded. On the one hand, it is a positive, almost incredible development that people with lengthy negative clinical files and measured intelligence that averaged about 30 for the first time received an opportunity to work in real jobs for real pay and integrated with predominantly nonhandicapped persons. The cumulative earnings of over $200,000 compares very favorably with a zero level total for those who are in adult activity centers or the very low subminimum wages usually earned in sheltered workshops. The ability to have such new disposable income can radically change lives as well as long-term outlook and freedom (Gersten, Crowell, & Bellamy, 1986). The total cost of services for these individuals was $97,000; Therefore, it can be seen that for each public dollar spent, over two dollars was earned by these workers. Although there are some vocational rehabilitation administrators who might not find this cost efficient, by and large, given the measured intelligence of this population and its historical earning power, this is a favorable outcome.

Most of these people had no previous work history; they had limited communication and travel skills, no academic skills, and most had not had the benefit of community-based programs in integrated schools. And now, even those who resigned or were terminated have an established work history on which to base future employment encounters. By using a supported employment approach, real work was obtained, causing a multitude of benefits to occur such as

1. the opportunity to interact with nonhandicapped people;
2. the opportunity to earn decent wages, pay taxes, etc.;

3. the opportunity to establish a work history for eventual advancement;
4. the opportunity for their families and others to view them in a competent role.

Data from supervisor evaluations, hours of on-site staff intervention and job retention suggest that these workers have the capability to succeed in competitive employment, assuming there is appropriate professional staff support, ongoing or intermittent, at the job site. This is highly encouraging since it further expands the base of knowledge from which current supported employment programs are now being developed and new programs and policies are being planned. Furthermore, it significantly complements the work done by the University of Oregon group (e. g., Mank et al., 1986) as well as numerous other state-of-the-art vocational programs nationally (e. g., Kiernan & Stark, 1986; Rusch, 1986). Specifically, it begins to document with more difficult populations how positive, paid, vocational outcomes can accrue.

It should be noted that there is a seeming incompatibility between the generally positive supervisor evaluations and the reasons given for job separation. The best explanation is that employers generally are reluctant to provide negative written feedback on workers with severe disabilities. Hence, a halo effect seems to have emerged.

There is a more sobering, less positive, side to these data as well. For example, many of the people, especially those at the school age level, were unable to get 35-40 hours of work per week. Also they were, for the most part, placed in entry-level service positions which some critics feel were demeaning. There is no question that significant job-coach support hours were necessary and will continue to be. It is evident that job retention of 55-60% is not what we would ultimately like to see. It is evident that only localities which offer this type of employment model will be able to make such vocational opportunities available. Therefore, if one is labeled as profoundly retarded and grows up in a particular part of the state or country, there may be no job for that person, although the vocational technology is clearly emerging which suggests otherwise. Furthermore, it should be noted that even though the people in the report had relatively low IQs, they did not have the serious ambulation or sensory problems of much of the population at large with severe and profound handicaps.

In closing, what can we say we have learned about this group? First, this report adds to and extends the accumulating evidence about the nonsheltered work potential of people with severe and profound retardation. It should be observed as well that if this study group was expanded to a population with IQs under 45 within our overall data bank (Hill et al., in press), would increase by another 50 clients. Second, social incompetence and inability to relate to nonhandicapped peers was a major problem of many of these 21 persons and caused separation. Thus more programs in integrated settings must be undertaken. Third, it is very evident to those closely involved in day-to-day supported competitive employment programs that job development and cultivation of the "right" job is more important than ever for people with complex learning problems. Finally, more knowledge is necessary in how to apply systematic behavioral instructional techniques in fast-paced nonsheltered work settings.

Clearly, major challenges lie ahead vocationally for these persons. It is important to expand our base of knowledge with similar programs involving persons with more profound handicaps in unique and innovative vocational arrangements.

References

Bates, P. & Panscofar, E. (1983). Project EARN. British Journal of Mental Subnormality, 7, 17-23.

Bellamy, G. T., Horner, R., & Inman, D. (1979). Vocational training for severely retarded adults. Baltimore: Paul Brookes, Inc.

Borbeau, P. (1985). Mobile work crews: An approach to achieve long term supported employment. In P. McCarthy, J. Everson, S. Moon, & M. Barcus (Eds.), School to work transition for youth with severe disabilities (pp. 151-166). Richmond, VA: Rehabilitation Research and Training Center.

Brown, L., Shiraga, B., Ford, A., VanDeventer, P., Nisbet, J., Loomis, R., & Sheet, M. (1984). Teaching severely handicapped students to perform meaningful work in nonsheltered vocational environments. In R. Morris & B. Blott (Eds.), Perspectives in Special Education. Glenview, IL: Scott Foresman, Co.

Elder, J. (1984). Job opportunities for developmentally disabled people. American Rehabilitation, 10(2), 26-30.

Gold, M. W. (1972). Stimulus factors in skill training of the retarded on a complex assembly task: Acquisition, transfer, and retention. American Journal of Mental Deficiency, 76, 517-526.

Hill, J., Banks, D., Hill, M., & Wehman, P. (in press). Individual characteristics and environmental effects on the competitive employment of workers with mental retardation. American Journal on Mental Deficiency.

Kiernan, W., & Stark, J. (Eds.). (1986). Pathway to employment. Baltimore: Paul Brookes, Inc.

Mank, D., Rhodes, L., & Bellamy, G. T. (1986). Four supported employment alternatives. In W. E. Kiernan and J. A. Stark (Eds.), Pathways to employment for adults with developmental disabilities (pp. 139-154). Baltimore: Paul Brookes, Inc.

Rhodes, L., & Valenta, L. (1985). Industry based supported employment. Journal of the Association for the Severely Handicapped, 10, 12-20.

Rusch, F. R. (1986). Competitive employment: Issues, theories, and models. Baltimore: Paul Brookes, Inc.

Rusch, F. & Mithaug, D. (1980). Vocational training for mentally retarded adults. Champaign, IL: Research Press.

Vogelsburg, R. T. (1985). Competitive employment programs for individuals with mental retardation in rural areas. In S. Moon, P. Goodall, and P. Wehman (Eds.), Critical issues related to supported employment (pp. 55-69). Richmond, VA: Rehabilitation Research and Training Center, Virginia Commonwealth University.

Wehman, P. (1981). Competitive employment: New horizons for severely disabled persons. Baltimore: Paul Brookes, Inc.

Wehman, P. (1986). Supported competitive employment for persons with severe disabilities. Journal of Applied Rehabilitiation Counseling, 18(1), 24-29.

Wehman, P., & Hill, J. (Eds.). (1985). Competitive employment for persons with mental retardation. Vol. I. Richmond, VA: Rehabilitation Research and Training Center, Virginia Commonwealth University.

Wehman, P., Hill, M., Hill, J., Brooke, V., Pendleton, P., & Britt, C. (1985). Competitive employment for persons with mental retardation: A follow-up after six years. Mental Retardation, 23, 274-281.

Will, M. (1984). Supported employment: An OSERS position paper. Washington, DC: U. S. Department of Education.

In Response to Paul Wehman and Janet W. Hill

A Look at the Need to Further Organize and Design Services

Kevin J. Lessard

During the past few years, I've had the opportunity to follow Paul Wehman's research and I would like to comment on the programmatic needs of individuals with profound handicaps with deafness and blindness within the context of his research and other areas of need. I would also like to address the development of transitional services for the population, as well as parents' rights and a further definition of accountability for professionals. I will also include some recommendations for future action and policy development.

The development of community-based services for individuals with deaf-blind handicaps is, without a doubt, our most critical challenge. It requires a redefinition of our professional accountability as we become actively involved in the development of community-based services. It requires us to become involved in complex networks of services and politics, both of which may be unfamiliar to us.

We need to develop a comprehensive continuum of services, given the wide functioning range of those who are deaf-blind, and we need to focus our attention on a housing as well as a vocational continuum.

Vocational training and vocational placement will make the difference in whether an individual who is handicapped with deafness-blindness is allowed to enter into a community-based housing program. This is true since very few residences have the operational monies to staff a program during traditional work hours.

When we analyze the evolution of services for these individuals, we can see the significant gains which have been made in the past five to ten years because of Title VI-C funding, Public Law 94-142, and state special educational legislation. The recent focus on transitional service has certainly helped these individuals, particularly those that are in the process of aging-out of the education system. Some of the positive features of research such as this done by Paul and other people in the field have had a positive impact on integrating these individuals into vocational and living options in the community.

Generally speaking, there has been a greater emphasis on developing community-based services. There has been a greater emphasis on more of a planned approach for these individuals, which includes direct instruction, transitional planning, and placement in meaningful employment. Another positive feature of the past few years has been the evolution of parents' rights, the clarification of parents' legal rights, and the development of a process in which parents have become involved as planners and coplanners with professionals.

These advances, however, have not been sufficient to ensure the development of a comprehensive system of services that will guarantee appropriate placements for the majority of these individuals. A number of problem areas continue to exist and they include the following variables:

A recent Harris Poll has shown that 66% of all disabled individuals are unemployed.
Disabled individuals are not necessarily guided into employment opportunities that are appropriate for their abilities.
Too much vocational training takes place in isolation and in a vacuum.
Systematic and planned transition to positions in business and industry are not usually available.
Communication between school personnel and adult service providers is typically limited.
Transportation systems and the availability of funds to pay for transportation services are limited in many parts of the country. In some cases, these limitations may dictate the particular placement of an individual.
Lack of contingency plans hinder clients when they are unable to go to work because of sickness or other factors.
The teacher shortage is becoming a national problem and some areas of the country are unable to provide minimal services.

When we analyze a continuum of vocational and work options, supported work options within business and industry are most attractive. How we develop an adequate array and a sufficient number of positions is critical, and what we do in the interim to maintain and stabilize a community-based placement for a client is also a factor that needs attention.

Paul mentions four particular benefits that were realized by having severely handicapped individuals become involved in competitive employment opportunities:

1. The opportunity to interact with nonhandicapped people.
2. The opportunity to earn reasonable wages and pay taxes.
3. The opportunity to establish a work history for eventual advancement.
4. The opportunity for their families and other people to view them in a competent role.

Even those who resigned or were terminated, now, for the first time, have an established work history from which to base future employment opportunities.

I would also like to comment on a number of other factors associated with integration into competitive employment placements. Data from Paul's study suggest that the workers have the ability to be successful in competitive employment, assuming there is appropriate professional staff support at the job site on an ongoing or intermittent basis.

In our community-based vocational programs at Perkins, we have identified a number of significant responsibilities that staff must assume if successful and continued affiliations are to be realized. In many cases these are new roles for our staff, and the biggest mistake we made when we first began placing students was in not identifying this full range of new responsibilities and, therefore, not training staff appropriately.

Staff who are developing or teaching in community-based programs must consider the following:

Continuous assessment of available community employment opportunities to expand job options and to protect clients in cases where businesses close or where lay-offs take place.

Awareness of the auditory and visual changes that can take place with these students who are deaf-blind and related medical implications of the etiology including but not limited to the onset of diabetes and the resulting medical and behavioral changes that can and will occur.

Knowledge of federal and state labor laws, as well as insurance factors that prospective employers always have regarding liability.

Training of teachers to gradually integrate a client into a competitive worksite. Orientation that is too short can be detrimental to the overall goal of training and eventual placement.

Communication with a blue collar supervisor who may have minimal sensitivity to the type of professional supervision to which the teacher is accustomed. Determining the supervisor's and nonhandicapped co-workers' work styles, work habits, and the general climate within the worksite is critical. Standards of cleanliness and other factors familiar to teachers may be dramatically different. While teachers need to support the clients, there will usually have to be some compromises.

Training of teachers regarding their separation from supervised and direct instruction. This can be difficult because the process is not taught in most undergraduate or graduate training programs. Difficulty in withdrawing from the teaching situation can negatively affect a client's program.

Determination by teachers of the time factors and the time frequencies relating to an individual's need for follow-up services and ongoing support.

Recognition of multiple safety factors in order for teachers to make recommendations to supervisors. Multiple safety factors can include the following:

Basic orientation and mobility techniques.

Adaptation of equipment to accommodate the auditory and visual needs of the client. Also knowing when to have a rehabilitation engineer oversee adaptive procedures.

An understanding of OSHA standards and policies.

Once successful placements are completed, not only is ongoing monitoring needed, but serious consideration should be given to appropriate recognition of companies and their employees. Public relations become important and there are many possibilities for recognition and awards that can help enhance relationships.

The expanded and new roles of teachers and trainees within business and industry cannot be underestimated, and a forum for discussion of problem areas and inservice training is critical in the process.

In analyzing future needs, I would emphasize consideration of the following recommendations:

1. We need more specialists trained in deaf-blind, multihandicapped education, who will be able to communicate effectively with students who are deaf-blind. Professionals need to be able to diagnose, evaluate, and design instructional techniques that accommodate an individual deaf-blind student's visual and/or auditory abilities and provide training that takes into account an expanding community-based curricula. Attention to different and complicated medical and behavioral problems is also critical.

2. We need more political and parental advocay, and we need to recognize and respect parents' abilities to change the system.

3. We need more cooperation between researchers and educational and rehabilitation personnel in the field of deaf-blindness.

4. We need better dissemination approaches and more creative ways of designing research so that the defensive posture taken by education and rehabilitation agencies against community-based services will be eliminated or significantly reduced. Many people do not know about innovative vocational training options.

5. It is difficult at this time to make a perfect placement--one in which all conditions are satisfied. There are too few community-based employment opportunities in business and industry at this time. Until such time as there are sufficient community-based vocational opportunities, do we support less desirable vocational options in sheltered settings if the placement and access to housing and support services are available and dependent on a day placement? Or do we wait until we can have the perfect setting? How much compromise is justified?

6. We need to look at vocational placements in the overall context of developing community-based services. We need to design ways to integrate housing options, vocational options, and medical and support services. The development of an integrated plan for one student requires a commitment on the part of many professionals from varied and different human service agencies, from the client, and, in particular, from parents who must be further educated to help them understand their roles and their rights. Parents, however, must also be assisted by professionals to understand and deal with the following:

    A lack of entitlement legislation.

    A lack of adequate financing.

    Too few housing, vocational, and support and medical services.

    The psychological dynamics associated with their child being placed within a system that is not as well coordinated as their child's educational programming.

    The dynamics associated with guardianship arrangements and the development of Estate and Trust Planning which automatically creates a clearer and greater sense of concern as they begin the process of developing long-term or life-long plans for their son or daughter.

7. We need to address all of the issues Paul mentioned as problem areas in his study. They include the following:

    Improvement of the retention rate of 55 percent to 60 percent.

    Ways to alter the negative factors of low production norms and poor endurance.

    More knowledge regarding how to apply systematic behavioral and instruction techniques in fast-paced, nonsheltered work settings. For example, the majority of the "rubella population" needs structure, since these persons have a tendency toward impulsivity, and they may react negatively to inconsistent supervision.

8. We need to have available appropriate sheltered employment opportunities for clients who fail in a competitive, supported work environment.

At Perkins, we recognize that the development of community-based service is a complex process. It is challenging and, at times, overwhelming. It is exciting and, at times, frustrating. Yet the more we become involved, the more we are convinced that the time, effort, and energy expended is truly worth it. We need to be ready to deal with the long-term and life-long care needs of those who have deaf-blind handicaps, especially those who are lower functioning.

In addition to advocacy, our efforts will also require funding, strong leadership, and the involvement of national, state, and local officials, as well as business and industrial leaders. Our efforts will require a commitment on the part of professionals to become planners, coplanners, and advocates within the public and private sectors.

Accountability is our professional responsibility and the individuals we serve and their parents depend very heavily on us to interpret and follow through on program design and implementation. How well we organize and design services and to what extent we become involved with the development of living and vocational options in the community and life-long care systems will determine our definitions and our commitment to the concept of accountability. In essence, it will determine the extent of our commitment to the individuals and the parents that we serve.

In Response to Paul Wehman and Janet W. Hill

The Vocational Rehabilitation Perspectives

Nancy Norman

We at the Iowa Commission for the Blind administer the vocational rehabilitation program for Iowans who are blind, and we operate an orientation center. We also operate one of the largest libraries to be found anywhere for those who are blind and physically handicapped.

Paul Wehman of the Rehabilitation Research and Training Center at Virginia Community University mentioned that there is now greater promotion of the entire employment movement for the disabled. Perhaps that is because there is generally such an emphasis on jobs. Farmers are concerned about jobs; the shoe industry is concerned about jobs. Manufacturing people are concerned that jobs are going to be exported to Mexico and Korea. The fabric of politics is changing. We are seeing changes in coalitions; constituencies are focusing their efforts, not so much in Washington any more, but back home in the states since President Reagan took office.

The basic knowledge about our programs for the blind and disabled has changed and increased. I would imagine that is because all of us now have some working knowledge of the computer, which has helped in the collection of data. The computer has aided persons such as Paul in doing more research.

The Iowa Commission for the Blind is charged by state statute with keeping a registry of those who are blind and in Iowa, that includes those that are deaf-blind. In Iowa, we know of individuals who are blind by the time they reach two years of age. We have long been concerned about transition from school to work; that is probably true of lots of agencies across this country. We know that eventually most of these children will become part of our vocational rehabilitation case load or part of our independent-

71

living case load, and we want to find out about these individuals as soon as possible. We are not greatly concerned with the IQ level of our clients because our first concern is assisting people who are blind. We do work with the two hospital-schools for the mentally retarded in Iowa, in order to keep tabs on those who are blind or deaf-blind in those institutions.

We have had some experience with supported work through a project with the Menninger Foundation, which has an agreement with a large hotel chain in Des Moines. We contracted with Easter Seals to provide the job coach. Unfortunately, the hotel changed hands and many of the personnel changed, so our experience was not conclusive regarding whether supported work would be successful. Nonetheless, we have entered that arena.

I, too, had the benefit of reading Paul's paper, and I read that paper as the crusty old administrator that I am. I have three questions that I would like to ask, not because I am critical of the issue of supported work, but because, if this paper was brought to me by a staff member or an advocate, I would need to ask these questions before I could implement a supported work program.

The paper talks about the workers and how they were evaluated. The evaluations in the paper are very favorable since most of the workers that were evaluated showed at least adequate and above-adequate performance. But when I looked at the reasons why individuals were no longer working, low-quality work, slow work, problems with attendance or tardiness, insubordination, aggressive behavior, and poor appearance were mentioned. Those appear to me to be in conflict with the actual evaluations that were shown in the paper. Also, over the eight-year time period, it appears that only eight of the twenty-one people worked for two years or more. I would like to know more about that.

Another area that I would like more information about is employer attitude. Supported work is a new initiative in many states and employers may be interested for that reason. What are seen as the long-range implications of this population entering the market place on the relationships, which have been established over time, between vocational rehabilitation agencies and employers?

The third question relates to cost. Many of us are probably aware that the Rehabilitation Act is up for reauthorization.[*] Supported work is probably the most controversial issue surrounding the whole reauthorization process, and it is controversial because of money. The fear on the part of administrators is that a great amount of staff time will need to be spent on coaching individuals. This is time that could be spent on finding jobs for individuals in other populations.

In his paper, Paul indicates that the twenty-one people in the study earned more than $208 thousand over the period of the study. If my calculations are correct, about $97 thousand was spent on job coaches. I would like to know what the $20 job-coach rate includes and if there are other costs included for determination of eligibility, administration, supervising of the job coaches, clerical computer time, and others.

Also, in your paper, and again today, Paul has mentioned that more creative and in-depth job development needs to be included or expanded in this project, and that perhaps there needs to be more training for clients. This was confusing since when I read it, I thought he referred to training before on-the-job training. I also thought that the social interaction of these people was, in many cases, the major reason why they were separated from their jobs. To me, that means that there needs to be more intense independent living services.

Those three add up to additional services. Thus, in my estimation, this program cannot be justified by numbers. It cannot be justified due to any significant pay back, and cost effectiveness is the strongest argument for vocational rehabilitation. However, supported work may be justified based on whether this employment made a difference in the quality of the lives of these people.

---

[*]Note: The Rehabilitation Act has since been reauthorized and includes provision for supported employment.

Report on the Working Group on Independent Living/Vocational Issues

Group Members

Rose Ceisla   Patricia McCallum
Mary Dickson   Beth Quarles
Sharon Freagon   Frank Simpson
Dorothy Hallett   Anne Smith
Kevin J. Lessard Philip Wade

Report prepared by Sharon Freagon and Kevin J. Lessard

This report shares the results of the working group on employment options for persons with deafness and blindness and severe multiple disabilities.

Belief Statement

1. We believe that as able-bodied, able-minded, and less-disabled planners that individuals who are profoundly multihandicapped with deafness and blindness have a right to dignity and their own pursuit of happiness and should not be placed in situations for the sake of placement.
2. We believe that each such individual deserves unlimited vocational options and choices, which should include supported employment and other varied work opportunities.
3. We believe that all employment options must be available to this population and that qualifed staff capable of providing adequate communication skills must be available to individuals to improve social integration and avoid any form of isolation.
4. Anyone working with individuals who are deaf and blind needs to be trained to diagnose, assess and design instructional techniques that take into account the

following areas:
a. auditory assessment and training;
b. visual assessment and training;
c. total communications approach;
d. orientation and mobility training;
e. self-preservation safety issues; and
f. systematic nonaversive behavioral instruction. This is essential for a majority of the rubella population that needs structure, realizing the tendency toward impulsivity and the negative reaction to inconsistent structure or changes within the environment.

5. Housing, employment, health, medical, and leisure and recreation needs are all interdependent.
6. Health issues must be considered in all work environments and as a part of the individual's service plan.
7. Early preparation, beginning at birth, for the world of living and work should include higher expectations while continuing to encourage the development of skills, experiences, attitudes, and community integration.

Service Delivery Approach

1. Development of resources at the local "grass roots" level is essential for the provision of effective vocational rehabilitation services.
2. The supported work concept should be accepted as a viable case closure and "marketed" to administrators.
3. There is a need to evaluate and improve existing work options, including, but not limited to, home-based options, day habilitation centers, work activity centers, sheltered workshops, industrial enclaves, and supported work environments in business and industry.
4. The evaluation of client progress should be broadened, and "success" redefined to include qualitative aspects of work-related behaviors (e.g. physical and social well-being, competence, variety, security, health, individual choice, and interactions).
5. Developing and implementing employment models nationwide should be viewed as a twofold process:
    a. strategies for those entering adult services without preparation for work, i. e., no educational preparation;
    b. strategies for those entering adult services with preparation for work, i. e., educational preparation.
6. Effective working relationships must be established between all agency programs for interagency cooperation/collaboration to assume/designate responsibility.
7. The effectiveness of the job coach model should be demonstrated with persons who possess a variety of handicaps using nonvisual and nonverbal techniques.
8. Implications of employment of handicapped persons should be studied in terms of the impact upon the nonhandicapped labor force. Regional variables and the economic climate should be considered.
9. Federal recognition of vocational rehabilitation eligibility should be obtained for this population. Parent education about supported employment should be as thorough as it was for Public Law 94-142. Parent involvement should be encouraged and their expertise should be utilized.
10. Additionally, there is a need for education of the general public and professional development strategies to heighten awareness, promote acceptance, and create positive changes in attitudes. Dissemination of information and research findings should be planned to lessen, not increase, resistance.

Issues and Considerations

These issues and considerations are organized into the following areas: (a) staffing and training, (b) federal, state, and local implications, (c) networking and interagency cooperation, and (d) parents and families.

Staffing and Training

1. Anyone working with deaf and blind populations needs to be trained to diagnose, assess, and design instructional techniques in the following areas:
   a. auditory assessment and training,
   b. visual assessment and training,
   c. total communication,
   d. orientation and mobility,
   e. self-preservation and safety,
   f. behavior, specifically the tendency of the rubella population to be impulsive and react negatively toward inconsistencies and changes in the environment.
2. There needs to be preservice and inservice training of personnel including regular education teachers, special education teachers and rehabilitation counselors to prepare them for their involvement in supported work programs.
3. The status of "Job Coach" in the supported work model needs to be elevated so quality people can be recruited for the position.
4. The state agencies need to work with universities to develop personnel training for the supported work model.
5. Improvement is needed in instructional, clinical, and research efforts addressing the following issues:
   a. placement techniques,
   b. retention problems,
   c. low production norms,
   d. poor endurance,
   e. family involvement.
6. Federal support is needed for deaf-blind and multihandicapped teacher training to address the national personnel shortage.

Federal, State, and Local Implications

1. There is a nationwide shortage of trained personnel to work with the identified population. We recommend federal support for training of teachers, counselors, vocational rehabilitation personnel and job coaches as well as for the provision of inservice training of existing personnel.
2. We recognize that there are presently some successful programs around the country. We recommend that the federal government identify the programs, the characteristics that make them successful, and the leaders of such programs to provide others the opportunity to identify the characteristics most applicable to their situation and determine potential for replicating the program.
3. It is imperative that an agency in each state be designated to assume the primary responsibility for coordinating case management for people who are in the identified population. Effective, active relationships need to be defined to provide interagency cooperation and collaboration.
4. In line with the above, effective shared funding responsibilities need to be outlined.
5. In order for Vocational Rehabilitation funding and services to be an integral part of transition, there needs to be a consistent federal interpretation of Vocational Rehabilitation eligibility for this population.
6. In addition, supported work needs to be recognized as a legitimate Vocational Rehabilitation closure, with the funding provided by Vocational Rehabilitation (or some other agency) to continue support services indefinitely. Also, supported work

needs to be "marketed" to program administrators as a valued and viable outcome, as opposed to just a "fad."

Networking and Interagency Cooperation

If Vocational Rehabilitation is only as good as local community resources, then active, local, "grassroots" development of those resources must continue and be expanded.

Parents and Families

1. Parents and families need appropriate education and training regarding the existing vocational rehabilitation systems and the new supported work concepts.
2. Ongoing parent/family counseling is needed that is geared toward preparing them for the possible future service/placement of their family member who is disabled.
3. Inclusion of parents and family expertise regarding the abilities and needs of their family member who is disabled is needed in the transition process.
4. Parent-to-parent training and sibling-to-sibling training should be utilized in the transition process.
5. Guardianship information, financial, estate, and trust planning expertise should be included as part of the total transition process.

Recommendations

1. The results of this national conference on the transition of profoundly multiply handicapped deaf and blind youth should be widely disseminated throughout the country and to multiple human service agencies.
2. OSERS should make a legislative and financial commitment to the major recommendations of this conference.
3. While supported work programs, other vocational options and related support services require a commitment on the part of local communities, also required is a significant federal effort to fund programs and projects throughout the country to demonstrate successful community-based program development possibilities.
4. Federal and state rehabilitation systems need to develop financial and other incentive programs to allow rehabilitation counselors a greater degree of latitude in designing and following through on long-term programs for individuals who are profoundly multiply handicapped and deaf and blind.
5. A nationwide strategy needs to be developed to ensure parents and family participation in the development of community-based housing, vocational, medical and recreation services and the development of life-long care systems for individuals who are profoundly multiply handicapped with deafness and blindness.
6. The development of future plans should include the participation of parents and professionals from the fields of deafness and blindness, the severely handicapped, and maternal and child health. Additional disciplines that need to be included are from the fields of autism, rehabilitation, health and human services, and developmental disabilities.

SECTION III.   HEALTH AND PSYCHOSOCIAL ASPECTS OF TRANSITION

Youth with Profound Multiple Handicaps of Deaf-Blindness:
Health Issues in Their Transition

Sharon L. Hostler

Introduction

During the 1964-65 rubella epidemic, 30,000 infants were born with congenital rubella syndrome (CRS) (Cooper, 1975). In 1969, the rubella vaccine was licensed. In 1985, only two infants with congenital rubella syndrome were reported to the Center for Disease Control (Morbidity and Mortality Weekly Report, Volume 35:9, March 7, 1986). In 1986, 6,023 profoundly multiply handicapped, deaf-blind survivors are aging out of the educational system into the community. What are the health care needs of these survivors and their families? What are the needs of the health care system? Where are the models of excellence in practice or in concept to meet the needs of survivors, families, and health care systems?

On the 24th of July, 1974, a conference on the future of deaf-blind children was conducted by the John Tracy Clinic and funded by the former Bureau of Education for the Handicapped. The title of that conference was 1980 IS NOW. The stated purpose was to stimulate planning to meet the individual and social needs of a projected 5,000 plus deaf-blind children from the 1964-65 rubella epidemic who would be maturing by 1980. The final five recommendations of the conference were as follows:

1. immediate initiation of planning efforts for services by 1980,
2. development of accurate definitions of "deaf-blind" and "rubella-child,"
3. call for a continuum of services from childhood through adulthood,
4. training of personnel,
5. development of a spectrum of model living and working styles for individuals who are deaf-blind (Lowell, 1974).

We are all aware that the projected continuum of services is not in place as of today, the seventh of April, 1986.

Health care was mentioned only briefly in the proceedings of that conference: hospitals were not good places for children to live (Rieger, 1974), and projected services should include premarital genetic counseling and rehabilitative therapy (Lowell, 1974). Why so little emphasis on health? By 1974, the morbidity and mortality peaks had passed. The emphasis legitimately shifted from medical to developmental concerns. The critical need to preserve residual functions of children with CRS was not fully appreciated in practice. The late sequelae of CRS did not appear in the published pediatric literature until 1975 (Cooper), although the 25-year experience of the 1940 epidemic in Australia had been reported elsewhere (Menser, Dods, & Harley, 1967). Issues of adolescence unique to special-needs teens became increasingly evident with the implementation of Public Law 94-142 guaranteeing education for all handicapped children from 3 to 21 years of age in the least restrictive setting. Today, not only does the implementation of Section 504 of the amended 1973 Rehabilitation Act ensure equal access to health care services, but our current concept of health promotes physical and psychological well-being, not just the absence of disease.

Service Needs of the Individual: Health

Planning

The individual's self-care strengths, his communication mode, and his social characteristics are primary determinants of his adult living situation. The intensity and frequency of required medical services will influence this decision. The health component of transition planning incorporates the individual's life experiences, his medical history, his current medical status, and a reasonable prediction for his future health needs. A wheelchair, a feeding gastrostomy tube, an intermittent catheterization program or an intractable seizure disorder contribute increasing degrees of restriction on the choice of residential setting.

Although health issues may not be the primary concern for the successful transition of the person with profound multiple handicaps of deaf-blindness or the primary concern of his family, the following four areas need to be addressed:

1. lifelong promotion of physical and psychological wellness;
2. continued management of the manifestations of CRS:
   a. impaired hearing,
   b. impaired vision secondary to glaucoma or cataracts,
   c. mental retardation,
   d. heart disease,
   e. cerebral palsy,
   f. the associated communication, learning and behavior disorders;
3. timely diagnosis of late onset sequelae of CRS (Sever, 1985):
   a. diabetes mellitus (Cooper, 1975; Shaver, 1983),
   b. thyroid dysfunction (Clarke, 1984; Cooper, Shaver, Bright, Rogol, & Nance, 1984),
   c. ocular damage (Boger, 1980),
   d. cardio-vascular disease (Sever, South, & Shaver, 1985),
   e. encephalitis (Townsend et al., 1975; Weil et al., 1975; Waxham & Wolinsky, 1984),
   f. others;
4. successful completion of the physical and psychological tasks of transition:
   a. reconciliation of one's hopes and the relevant realities,
   b. modification of realities when possible,
   c. change of setting, program and team members,
   d. changing social and sexual roles of the young adult,
   e. obligatory grieving of the losses inherent in even positive change (Wheelis, 1973).

Today I would like to propose a process to identify the individual's health needs. The process includes four stages: (a) planning or needs assessment, (b) health assessment, (c) development of an adult health care program, and (d) family consultation. The time requirement for completion might vary from 6 to 12 months. In addition to family members, the specific disciplines and agencies involved will reflect the unique history of the youth and the community systems involved in his past and future.

Ideally, the transition planning would be initiated early in childhood so all intervention would be directly focused on adult outcome. Such a plan would necesarily be modified on a periodic basis as a result of changes in the child, his family, and his eventual community. In reality, the stress of managing immediate crises and coping "one day at a time" negates this ideal.

Transitions to a new stage in life are the periods of the greatest stress (Terkelsen, 1980). Families experience increased vulnerability during periods when their child enters or leaves school. Planning for transition necessitates clarification of family values. One intervention program identified these planning tasks for families: (a) identifying the quality-of-life criteria that are important, (b) identifying preferences of their son or daughter, (c) conducting ecological inventories of community programs, (d) evaluating alternatives against quality-of-life criteria, and (e) establishing priorities (Turnbull & Summers, 1985). Families are richly diverse and not all may value or participate in transition planning!

Transition Health Assessment

In preparation for the transition health assessment, a complete health record is compiled. Information gathering includes

1. all past health documents such as private office and clinic records, dental records, hospital discharge summaries, operative reports, lab results, x-rays, EKGs, audiograms, school records, emergency room records, mental health/behavioral psychology reports;

2. a current health profile including information on communication, mobility, feeding, self-care, medications, behavioral programs, therapy plans, the communication system, mobility devices, bowel and bladder programs, and updated family medical history;
3. a review of symptoms and concerns of caretaker, school and family.

Information gathering may be performed by any one of the team, for example, public health nurse, school nurse or case manager. The actual assessment process includes a review and summary of the information gathered; additional history-taking as indicated; the complete physical examination; appropriate work-up as indicated by the history and physical examination such as blood studies, audiograms, x-rays, or a subspecialty consultation; and a final document which summarizes all the above and projects future medical needs.

The health assessment is performed by the primary pediatrician who is committed to the care of this youth and his family. Although the primary pediatrician may have cared for the young adult from birth, it is doubtful that he or she has systematically reviewed all of his documentation or had access to a complete set of records. The process of review and summarization is very time-consuming, as we discovered in our own adolescent project. For example, the time required to review all the complex documentation of an 11-year-old girl with cerebral palsy was nine hours. This is an important procedure, no matter how well coordinated the health care delivery may have been. Appropriate incentives need to be provided to ensure its completion.

Attention is addressed to the progression and patterns of illness. Accidents, injuries, and behavioral changes need to be assessed in light of physical or sexual abuse. Immunizations may need to be updated. The medication profile is evaluated for the potential of drug elimination or simplification, reduction of side effects or long-term risks, cost reduction, a less intrusive schedule, an alternate route of administration, and abuse/dependency prevention. The family's medical history is reviewed for risk factors pertinent to the young adult's future health. For example, a family history of early onset coronary artery disease or rectal carcinoma would alter the projected medical screening.

The physical evaluation of the young adult has added value and efficiency when preceded by a thorough historical review. The specific content of a physical examination is dependent on the patient, the presenting issues, the examiner and their historical relationship. However, I believe the uniqueness of this health assessment dictates special attention to at least the following areas.

General Wellness

Height, weight, nutrition:
   sleep and eating patterns;
   adequate growth;
   unexplained changes in the growth curve;
   complete secondary sexual development;
   onset menses, cycle pattern;
   adequate dietary intake;
   increased fiber to eliminate laxative use;
   need for nutritional consultation;
   need for supplementation such as iron or calcium;
   immunization needs;
   indication for hemoglobin, hemocrit, and white blood cell count.

Two cases of growth hormone deficiency have been reported in CRS with the onset at 12 years in one boy (Preece, Kearney, & Marshall, 1977). Persistence of some growth slowing is indicated in the 1985 description of a CRS cohort of adolescents as "small and light" (Desmond, 1985) although well proportioned weight for height. Obesity, on the other hand, is an issue reported in group homes for the severely mentally retarded (Green & McIntosh, 1985).

Dental examination:
oral hygiene;
eruption complete, status of wisdom teeth;
adequate occlusion for speech, feeding, and attractiveness;
need for restoration or operative procedures;
does bruxism indicate need for protective device

Skin care:
hygiene, corns, infected nails;
decubiti, could acne care be improved;
evidence of self-stimulation or physical abuse.

Aspects Pertinent to the CRS

Hearing
evidence of excessive cerumen, ear infection, foreign body;
audiological assessment including review of aid appropriateness;
otologist referral.

The hearing loss associated with CRS may worsen as a complication of conductive problems and progresion of the sensorineural damage (Desmond et al., 1985). The latest age for progression documented is 10 years (Sever et al., 1985).

Vision
acuity; if glasses, an appropriate prescription;
if glasses, are they still intact;
intraocular pressure;
conjunctivitis;
retinal changes or injury;
ophthalmologic consultation.

Boger reports additional ocular damage in nearly 10% of children followed with CRS. The diagnosis of late onset glaucoma has been documented up to 22 years of age (Boger, 1980). A decrease in central vision has been related to subretinal neovascularization and reported to occur during years 8-17 (Frank & Purnell, 1978).

Communication:
current method, functional level;
with whom does he routinely communicate;
who is his interpreter in his current setting;
interpretive source in medical setting;
indicators of pleasure and pain;
most effective comfortconsoling measure;
appropriateness of communication system.

Feeding:
self; assisted or adapted;
intake adequate;
time requirement acceptable;
progress socially acceptable, in the community;
nasogastric or gastric tube feeding;

vomiting, self-stimulation;
drug side-effect;
aspiration pneumonia.

Mobility:
level of ambulation, injuries;
full range of motion at all joints;
special attention to the hips and knees of chair sitters;
more than 20 degrees of scoliosis;
patterns of spasm, need for continued medication;
orthoses still functional;
reduction in size or weight as appropriate;
updated adaptive devices;
electric or sport-weight chairs;
leisure and exercise;
therapeutic recreation;
medication; therapy needs;
orthopedic surgery.

Cardiac status:
activity level;
blood pressure;
history of risk factors;
change in history or physical findings.

Although congenital heart disease was a prominent concern during the early life of children with CRS, only one adolescent with functional heart disease was identified in a follow up study of 36 CRS teens with congenital heart disease as infants (Desmond et al., 1985). A second longitudinal study did not list cardiac disease as a long-term problem (Appell, 1985). Ligation of the patent ductus arteriosus has not been associated with late onset sequelae. If there is pulmonic valvular disease, one might consider an EKG and chest x-ray. If there is evidence of right ventricular hypertrophy, a cardiology consultation is indicated (H. P. Gutgesell, personal communication, 1986). Late appearance of hypertension has been described and concern stated that the vascular lesions of rubella may cause coronary, cerebral, and peripheral vascular disease in adulthood (Sever et al., 1985).

Diabetes Mellitus:
weight change;
increased thirst;
increased voiding;
bed wetting;
urinalysis;
hemoglobin A_1.

The association of diabetes mellitus with CRS was first reported in 1967 (Menser et al.) and confirmed in a 1975, ten-year follow-up of youngsters with CRS from New York (Cooper, 1975). The follow-up studies of the 1941 rubella epidemic in Australia indicated up to 20% had overt or latent diabetes mellitus by age 35 (Menser, Forest, Bransby, & Hudson, 1982). A current study of young adults with CRS is finding the occurrence of diabetes mellitus to be 1-2% with autoimmunity as the probable mechanism. There is not, to date, a clear pattern with respect to insulin dependence or age of onset. (Shaver, 1983; Clarke et al., 1984).

Thyroid function:
  serum for thyroid antibodies;
  if positive, then full thyroid function studies

In a study of adymptomatic adolescents with CRS between the ages of 15 and 18, 25% had demonstrated thyroid antibodies and 5% had thyroid dysfunction (Clarke et al., 1984).

Neurological evaluation:
  vision, hearing, mobility as above;
  change in frequency or form of seizures;
  appropriate blood levels of anticonvulsants;
  EEG;
  fine tuning of medications: simplification, reduction;
  side effects;
  injuries secondary to seizure activity;
  change in mental status, loss of skills;
  deterioration on neurological exam.

In 1975, progressive panencephalitis was reported in four patients with CRS with onset during adolescence and leading to death in two patients (Townsend et al., 1975; Weil et al., 1975). In total, 12 cases of fatal progressive rubella panencephalitis have been reported. All were boys who experienced the onset in their second decade with progressive neurological deterioration over 8 to 10 years (Waxham & Wolinsky, 1984).

Behavioral disorders:
  attention-seeking behavior;
  autism;
  temper-tantrums, self-stimulation;
  aggression;
  known aversive stimuli;
  eating or sleeping disorders;
  what is the behavior management strategy, does it generalize;
  are behaviors related to medication, time of day, activity.

Issues Related to Transition

Body image:
  need for visible devices;
  grooming level;
  family, staff or community concerns;

Socialization:
  friends, communication, conversation;
  preferred person, favorite object;
  roommate preference;
  recreation and leisure activity;
  possible lifting of outdated medical prohibitions;
  dress or undress alone, toilet independently;
  seductive behavior.

Sexuality:
  review of family values;
  level of sex education;
  body parts, relationship issues;

history of sexual activity;
private vs. public behaviors;
personal hygiene;
masturbation, sexual activity, other;
personal hygiene ability;
pregnancy and veneral disease prevention;
behavioral or pharmacologic prevention;
sterilization.

The incidence of sexual activity in a group of 108 moderately to severely physically disabled adolescents of ages 13-18 was 17% (Hostler & Linden, 1981). Depo-Provera, 150-250 mg every three months, usually prevents ovulation. Sterilization using federal funds since the moratorium of 1973 is prohibited. Sterilization is available with adjudication of the youth as incompetent in most states with the assignments of a guardian ad litem for the youth and legal representation for the parents.

Examination:
    breast exam, pelvic exam, Pap smear;
    vaginal discharge, infection;
    foreign body, hernia, phimosis;
    testicular masses.

Safety:
    accident pattern;
    self-abuse;
    drug overdose;
    molestation, rape, physical abuse;
    environmental requirements;
    supervision requirements.

In a 1970 report, 29% of the 6,000 abused children had developmental disabilities prior to abuse (Gil). A survey of Parents' Anonymous members revealed that 58% of their abused children had "developmental problems" (Chotiner & Lehr, 1976). The 1979 data fo the National center on Child Abuse and Neglect indicated that 16.3% of all substantiated reports involved children with special charateristics as opposed to the incidence of 7-10% of children with disability (Mattsoon, 1972). Episodes of sexual molestation and rape of the disabled are discussed among parents in quiet desperation, although the incidence of sexual abuse is not known. Concern about the incidence of sexual abuse is not known. Concern about the incidence of accidents and suicide was noted in two recently published longitudinal studies of the CRS population (Desmond et al., 1985; Appell, 1985).

Separation:
    family members' reaction to anticipated change;
    projection of youth's awareness of setting, structure, and caretaker change;
    immediate need for intervention or counseling referral for any family member;
    how else can the physician be helpful;
    timely report, support;
    legal or funding help;
    identification of community resources;
    competent and caring health professionals;
    is the physician "letting go" successfully.

Independence:
    rehabilitation engineers;
    architectural recommendations for deaf-blind residences;
    assistive devices;
    lifts, ramps, bumpers;
    transportation needs;
    sheltered workshop.

Alarm systems with flashing lights and vibration are well known for this population. The potental of flashing lights to precipitate seizures must be remembered, especially at this period when anticonvulsants may have been decreased or eliminated. Environmental controls are successfully used by severely mentally and physically handicapped persons. Robots have been developed at Johns Hopkins and UCLA with the capability of feeding (Cain, 1985). Possibilities of neuroprostheses or sensory prostheses are currently being researched (Desch, 1986). The Mowak sensor (a hand-held mobility aid using a narrow beam of reflected high intensity light that produces vibration in the sensor when the sound is reflecting from an object) and the Sonic Guide are in limited use (Mellor, 1984). Assistive devices and electronic communication aides are exciting but require very prescriptive trials with the individual client in his specific setting to demonstrate functional usefulness. Artificial intelligence, robotics, interactive video simulations, and telecommunication systems may have practical value in the near future (Cain, 1985).

The physician compiles, in a timely manner, the formulation of the medical history, physical exam, and consultations into a concise document, and makes specific recommendations for inclusion in the adult care plan.

Adult Care Plan

The family and the designated transition team work together to develop the lifelong health care plan. Transition stresses the families. It also stresses those school, pediatric, or other developmental professionals who must alter or relinquish their helping roles. A family's wish to continue contact with a favorite provider (often the ophthalmologist) should be honored. A successful bridge to the community requires very precise descriptions of services needed and clearly stated limits of acceptability. The "child-team members" must be open to flexible, segmented, nonfamiliar, and even nontraditional patterns of service delivery. Once again, value clarification, priority establishment, and compromise are critical. Clear and honest communication is essential between the child and the adult health care teams.

The adult care plan includes provisions for wellness promotion, management of current health problems, intercurrent care and critical care. Wellness promotion includes optimal nutrition, dental care, fitness prescription (endurance, flexibility, strength), communication, safety, accident prevention, and socialization. If hearing was stable at the transition assessment, then scheduled audiological evaluation should occur every 18-24 months to ensure aids are functioning. If fluctuating hearing or loss of hearing is documented, then the interval should be every three months. A visual acuity and intra-ovular pressure measurement schedule is developed according to the individual's needs. The annual complete physical examination will necessarily include appropriate screening studies indicated by the CRS (hemoglobin A_1 and thyroid antibody screens), family history, and the patient's age.

The prescribed management of current health issues would be a direct follow-up of the transition assessment. Three examples of sample plans follow:

Dental:
    fluoride supplement in water source;
    limit high carbohydrate, occlusive snacks to once weekly;

self-brushing after each meal;

caretaker brushing once daily;

hygiene appointment every six months;

dental consultation yearly;

be sure that the preferred provider has accessible office and specific skills for dentistry for the disabled.

Sexuality (young woman):

personal hygiene program generalized;

behavior modification program continues regarding privacy requirement for masturbation (baseline frequency once monthly in public);

Depo-Provera 250 mg every three months to prevent pregnancy;

breast exam, pelvic exam, Pap smear, and review of Depo-Provera;

strong family history of breast cancer indicating need for baseline mammogram at age 35 years;

be sure that the preferred provider is woman gynecologist with accessible office in community.

Hearing:

if stable at transition health assessment, then audiologic evaluation to ensure aids are still functioning every 18 to 24 months;

if fluctuating or a loss is documented, then audiologic evaluation required every three months;

current equipment description, maintenance, reference and source;

be sure that the preferred provider is an otologist or audiologist with medical referral available

Intercurrent and critical medical care may be provided by various combinations of private, public, and university settings. The hierarchy of possible services ranges from a visiting public health nurse to a neighborhood practice or a regional emergency room. Historically, deinstitutionalized mentally retarded young adults have utilized primary care services more intensely than the control population (Schor, Smalky, & Neff, 1981). Means of transportation and the designated interpreter are identified. Severity of illness may require the primary practitioner to utilize a consultant, a laboratory facility or an inpatient hospital admission. High value is placed on the comfort of the patient, consistency of caretaker, and an efficient outpatient evaluation where possible. Appropriate hospital staff will receive preadmission training if admission is necessary. Environmental consistency will be sought. A family member or caretaker-advocate will be present as counselor and interpreter throughout all procedures and through anesthesia induction in the case of surgery. Issues of informed consent, patient advocacy, decision-making, funding responsibilities and discharge planning will occur in accordance with the plan and be reviewed prior to admission.

Advance planning for critical care demands identification of both an emergency transport system and preferred tertiary level emergency room and intensive care unit. A normal life span is expected. Predictable issues such as the right to treatment, resuscitation, extraordinary life supports, experimental therapy, painful procedures (bronchoscopy, cardiac catheterization), research participation, and terminal care require discussion and clarification. Even decisions regarding autopsy, organ donation, cremation, and/or interment are integral to the life planning process.

Families are confronted with an endless continuum of parental responsibility for a young adult who will always remain dependent. After years of a stable routine, changes occur along all the dimensions: new setting, new program, new staff. There will be different community adult vocational and rehabilitation programs. There will be Social Security Supplemental Income, Medicaid, guardianships, wills, trusts, legal, and ethical decisions. As the transition process evolves, families are asked both to make very immediate decisions about today's program and to project decisions beyond their own deaths.

The summary document of the transition health assessment is shared with the family and distributed throughout the identified health care network from visiting nurse to regional transport system. It includes not only the identified present and future health needs, but an action plan to meet those needs. The front of this document is a one-page profile of critical data for this young adult. After the necessary identification information, the medical content lists diagnostic categories, functional levels, height, weight, blood pressure, visual acuity, ocular pressure, audiologic information, medication detail, allergies, and identified risk factors. The psychological content includes the responsible caretaker-advocate or family member, communication mode, interpreter's name and phone number, comfort and pain indicators. The final section includes the funding documentation and the designated community health network. Responsibility for the ongoing update of the information in this document rests with the caretaker-advocate. Modification of the lifelong health strategy plan requires a combination of the family, the primary physician, and the caretaker-advocate.

Although there are health care issues to be addressed during this transition process, we must remember that caring relationships are far more essential to the young adult's well-being than any medical service. Health care services today are indeed portable and can be delivered to his or her setting. Decisions regarding medical services are secondary to finding a home.

Family Interpretive

Genetic counseling has been routinely provided to families of children affected with genetic diseases, handicapped school leavers (Vowles, 1981) and deaf students (Warren, Gallien, & Porter, 1982). There are few models for counseling of the brothers, sisters, parents and cousins of a youth who is profoundly handicapped with deafness and blindness. The time immediately following completion of the transition health assessment is very appropriate to share medical information. Siblings and parents may still have many unanswered questions about CRS. All those family members entering childbearing years have the right to information. Our experience with the format of the adolescent interpretive interview with 11-14-year-olds with physical disabilities and chronic illness affirms the richness of interest even in the absence of traditional indications for genetic counseling. The disability is viewed in a social context. Myths and misconceptions abound (Hassler & Hostler, 1986). Preparation, attention to process and content, privacy, and adequate time allotment are critical to a successful interpretive session. The interpretive conference can serve as the safe forum for the issues of life expectancy, future caretaking responsibility, and recognition of the role for all family members.

Service Needs of the Family: Psychosocial

What are the needs of the survivor families? And they are, in fact, survivors! The families themselves are best qualified to identify their own service needs, and Mary O'Donnell in her reaction to this paper (included in this book) will provide the expert testimony for this session. Forty-eight parents with children at the stage of transition from school to adulthood identified residential placements for their children as the greatest need (Turnbull & Summers, 1985). The parents of physically disabled adolescents receiving inpatient care at the Children's Rehabilitation Center listed the "return of their dignity" as the greatest need. This is in sharp contrast with the earlier stated needs for respite and discrete services (Tarran, 1981). Stress often increases with the age of the child (Gallagher, Beckman, & Cross, 1983). One study found parents of older children were less supported and more in need of expanded services (Suelzle & Keenan, 1981).

A "Family State-of-the-Art" Conference in February, 1986, was sponsored by the Office of Special Education and the Division of Maternal and Child Health. A list of needs generated by that parent-professional group included hope, control, power, friendship, choice, self-worth, privacy, respect for one's uniqueness, freedom from guilt, respite, leisure, personal growth, the permission to exclude the special child, trust in service providers, elimination of "placement" from the language, enactment of Medicaid amendments for residential life in the community, payment of family members as health care providers and more. The full proceedings have been edited by Dr. Ann Turnbull for an April 1986 distribution. I look forward to hearing Mary O'Donnell's experience with the New Jersey Association of Deaf-Blind and the comments of other parents here to identify the needs of families.

The resilience of families is truly astonishing. Their steadiness is especially commendable in this period of continual philosophical shifts among professionals shifting from segregated regional centers to integrated mainstreaming; as well as trying out oral, manual, total, and augmentative modes of communication. In the lifetime of these young adults, the system's view of families has evolved from seeing the family as the cause of the problem to having a parenting deficit to responsibility as a parent-teacher, to taking responsibilities as lobbyists, to becoming decision-makers, and, finally, to becoming the architects of the deaf-blind group home movement. A particular difficulty has been the system's inability to keep up with the changing nature and needs of families over the life cycle.

At the time these families had young children, the literature was filled with descriptions of what is wrong with families with handicapped children (Bryne & Cunningham, 1985). Today, however, researchers such as Dr. Vincent of the University of Wisconsin report that the data-based research since 1980, while indeed describing increased stress in families with handicapped children, does not describe the increased dysfunction (Pans, Brown, & Vincent, 1986) such as the increased divorce and suicide rates reported with families of mentally retarded children (Price-Bonham & Addison, 1978). Are these families coping better than regular families? Heresy! In fact, the current model of research activity seeks to discover how these same families cope and adapt to stress (Crnic, Friedrich, & Greenberg, 1983). While professionals and policy makers have been struggling with developing a conceptual model, most families have reared their deaf-blind child—sometimes with the support of the system, and sometimes in spite of the system.

Families form a diverse group with different sizes, shapes, and beliefs. An example is the strong family pride of Mexican-American families who reject outside help and prefer home care (Adkins & Young, 1976). Very few households meet the traditional model of mom, dad and two children, all biologically related. The 1980 census, in fact, reports only nine percent of households meet these strict criteria. And families who participate in national conferences are probably not representative of all the families. Consequently, flexible options for services are needed to reflect the rich differences in families and their values. Supported home care (Cina & Caro, 1984), nursing homes or hospices may be preferred by some families to the model of community-based residence.

Change in any one member of a family affects everyone else in the family. No one member is more important than another and all strive to have their needs met. All families experience the crisis times in the "letting go" process involved in parenting an adolescent (Minuchin, 1974; Simon, 1982). Most families have many opportunities to practice letting go—the curfew, the mohawk, the driver's license—before the move away from home. The sameness of the profoundly handicapped youngster precludes many of these practicing exercises. There are fewer ceremonial markers (graduations, weddings) for this kind of rite of passage. Even when the actual move to a group home is an overwhelming success, there may be tremendous feelings of loss and sadness in all family members. The transition may awaken the brother's worry about who will be caretaker after his parents' death, the sister's worry that her pregnancy may be problematic, or the parents' grieving. Extended family members and neighbors may not appreciate the sadness and may seem insensitive and unsupportive. The family may experience what Peck calls a "little death" before it reestablishes its balance and, with time, translates the pain into growth (1978).

How can the system support all family members in this transition? First, by remembering that all families have coping strengths and resources. Families successfully use the following coping strategies to reduce feelings of stress: (a) passive appraisal ("time for a bubble bath"), (b) reframing ("grass is browner"), (c) spiritual support ("my special child"), (d) social support ("without my hubby . . . "), and (e) professional support. Practice exercises for building coping strength have been compiled in a family self-help manual (Goldfarb, Brotherson, Summers, & Turnbull, 1986).

In Brotherson's interviews with 48 parents of transition aged children, she found the most important strategy for coping with future planning was reframing. Consultation with professionals ranked equally with alcohol, cigarettes, and TV and only slightly above medications as the most important coping strategy (Turnbull & Summers, 1985). In light of those findings, perhaps the health system might offer real social supports such as opening clinics to birthday parties, reunions, weddings, and other simple social events (Haggerty, 1980). Possibly the most important service the system can provide parents is not to become an additional source of stress (Turnbull & Turnbull, 1978). As Dr. Ann Turnbull exhorted at a recent conference: "Ask first not what families can do for the service delivery system but what the service delivery system can do for families."

Needs of the Health Care System

What are the needs of the health care delivery system? The system needs organization at a community and national level for anticipation of predictable crises, information exchange, resource sharing, technical assistance, and appropriate support to meet the stated needs of the individual and his family. Individual providers need communication skills, integrated service networks, consultation, and access to the informational systems. A wish of the system might be to rewrite the history of the past 21 years in such a way that transition planning had been mandated and all activities prior to transition had focused on "survival" life training. If, for life to have value, as Freud suggested, the primary needs of all individuals are to work and to love, then survivorship programming would have included early socialization, sexuality, and prevocational training.

First, let us discuss the communication skills needed by the individual providers, specifically, the physician. Pediatricians are accustomed to caring for patients who do not talk and who need a grown-up to take care of them. That is neither the expectation, training, or experience of the adult practitioner. Parents of disabled children have even been critical of some pediatricians' inability to communicate. The concept of a health care team within the hospital is better understood. Adult physicians participate in health teams primarily in rehabilitative, psychiatric and geriatric settings.

In the special education literature (Wolraich, 1982; Gallagher et al., 1982) and the pediatric literature (Taft, Matthews, & Molnar, 1984; Martin, 1985), specific characteristics of successful physician-parent interaction have been identified. Effective physicians demonstrate the art of communication. They listen as well as they talk. They possess adequate knowledge of the disability. Or they seek out essential information. Parents of disabled children have long described their frustration at the need to become an expert on their children because service providers were not well informed. Effective practitioners also exhibit positive atttitudes toward the child with a disability (he calls her by name) (Armstrong, Jones, Race, & Ruddock, 1980). The practical interactional skills needed by all providers include allowing enough time for health care interaction, learning how to use an interpreter, and gaining patience to delay doing the procedure until it has been explained. (Are these characteristics inate?)

How do we meet the needs for improved communication skills among the practioners?

Many medical schools have introduced courses and experiences to teach interpersonal skills and the social aspects of disease and disability. Economic forces are creating a different disability. Economic forces are creating a different medical school applicant. They are choosing medicine because of the cooperative role, the increased flexibility in practice styles and maybe even idealism. Nearly half the entering classes are now women--hopefully a caring and nurturing group! At best, training produces changes in behaviors but probably not changes in values and beliefs. The latter requires sequential affirming experiences to challenge and modify beliefs.

To create the numbers of physicians necessary today to care for this population means identifying the community practitioners with compatible value systems. The increasing numbers of physically disabled, mentally handicapped, and chronically ill adolescents entering the adult world will change the internist's medical as well as social experiences. Hopefully the behavior of younger graduates will reflect their training and idealism.

The individual provider, especially the physician, needs to develop communication skills with the other community members of the integrated service network. Practitioners learn team behaviors in sports, family life, medical school, hospital training, and on-the-job experience in the community. Successful teamwork demands structured interaction as well as timely reaction in crisis. The identified link person or caretaker-advocate must have ready access to and respect of the system. Patient-related success and a broadened world view are compensations for loss of time, money, and control. Appreciation of the contribution of the ASPCA volunteer or the recreational therapist simply takes experience. Others will never learn.

All community professionals need access to specific materials for sexuality training or training videotapes for hospital personnel, and expert consultation over confusing aspects of care for those who are deaf-blind. Access to the new technology must include trial periods with the clients. A lending library of training resources and a clearinghouse of helpful devices could serve a regional area.

The wants of the service delivery system are as important as its needs. Individual providers want to be valued. Professionals expect reasonable compensation for services. Quality services are not obtained as "favors" or charity. Not only do professionals want comfort and control in their lives, they also want joy and meaning. A conscious remodeling of our community interaction framework could meet both the needs and the wants of all involved.

On a national level, a network is needed for an appropriate exchange of successful problem-solving, innovative materials, and rare services such as psychiatric services for deaf-blind individuals. I propose establishing a periodic regional national conference with a mechanism for dissemination of the rich experiences resulting from work with this population to other parents and professionals.

On a societal level, a provision is needed for developmental services from cradle to grave, the right to live and work in a community, and the right to health-sustaining and other services. We need simplification of legal procedures, guardianships, wills and trusts, and a mechanism of peer review of all providers of services. We need flexible uses of health care dollars. We need Medicaid waivers to maintain our activities in the community, and we need access to the recreational arenas (swimming pools, parks) and transportation systems.

In sum, public policy must reflect responsibility for ensuring each person's right to health. Professional leadership such as we have at this conference can influence policy, can look beyond the present to see the future, can use knowledge to create solutions, and can muster the courage to act when others think it immoral, illegal, or impossible to act.

Over two million youngsters under the age of seventeen experience some degree of limitation in their school, play or other recreational activities because of chronic conditions (Newacheck, Budetti, & Halfon, 1986). The health care system needs a stimulus to achieve excellence. Excellence in the problem-solving for this population with profound, multiple handicaps of deafness and blindness can be translated into a whole spectrum of available services.

Conclusion

Let us review. We have discussed the specific health concerns for the young adult with profound multiple handicaps of deaf-blindness. A care plan must include provisions for wellness promotion, management of existing problems, screening for late onset sequelae, and periodic reevaluation of the plan with special attention to the usefulness of new technologies. Transition necessarily highlights issues and decisions regarding sexuality, independence, and separation.

As periods of transition are the periods of greatest stress, it is reasonable to expect family members and even systems to react. Parents, brothers, and sisters have issues. Families have different values and styles of coping, and these family differences demand flexible options. At the very least, the system should not add to family stress.

The health care system primarily needs a clearinghouse of resources and information organized at the local and national level. Participation in community health teams will require new communication skills. Model programs and practices are few but are sufficient to serve as a foundation. Services are portable and can follow the child into the community.

The well-being of the young adult is more related to caring relationships than to provision of medical services. To my fellow physicians, I offer the challenges of sharing risk-taking, the same risk-taking we ask of parents and of communities.

References

Adkins, P., & Young, R. G. (1986). Cultural perceptions in the treatment of handicapped school children of Mexican American heritage. Res Dev Educ, 9, 83-90.

Appell, M. W. (1985). The multi-handicapped child with congenital rubella: Impact on family and community. Rev Infect Dis, 7(1), 17-21.

Armstrong, G., Jones, G., Race, D., & Ruddock, J. (1980). Mentally handicapped under-fives: Needs and Sheffield services as seen by parents (ERG Rep. No. 8). University of Sheffield Evaluation Research Group.

Boger, W. P. (1980). Late ocular complications in congenital rubella syndrome. Ophthalmology, 87, 1244-1252.

Bryne, E. A., & Cunningham, C. C. (1985). The effects of mentally handicapped children on families—a conceptual view. J Child Psychology, 26, 847-864.

Cain, E. J. (1985, November). The present is the only prologue—the potential of technologies. Presentation at Computer Technology for the Handicapped, Minneapolis, Minnesota.

Chotiner, H., & Lehr, W. (Eds.). (1976). Child abuse and developmental disabilities. A report from the New England Regional Conference, sponsored by the United Cerebral Palsy Association.

Cina, S., & Caro, F. G. (1984). Supporting families who care for severely disabled children at home: A public policy perspective. Prepared for Community Service Society of New York.

Clarke, W., Shaver, K., Bright, G., Rogol, A., & Nance, W. (1984). Autoimmunity in the congenital rubella syndrome. J Peds, 104, 370-373.

Cooper, L. Z. (1975). Congenital rubella in the United States. In S. Krugman & A. Gershon (Eds.), Infections of the Fetus and the Newborn Infant (pp. 1-22). New York: Alan R. Liss.

Crnic, K. A., Friedrich, W. N., & Greenberg, M. T. (1983). Adaptation of families with mentally retarded children: A model of stress, coping and family ecology. Am J Ment Def, 88, 125-128.

Crowley, M., Keane, K., & Needham, S. C. (1982). Fathers: The forgotten parents. Am Ann Deaf, 127(1), 38-40.

Desch, L. W. (1986). High technology for handicapped children: A pediatrician's point of view. Pediatrics, 77, 71-86.

Desmond, M. M., Wilson, G. S., Vorderman, A. L., Murphy, M. A., Thurber, S., Fisher, E. S., & Krovlik, E. M. (1985). The health and educational status of adolescents with congenital rubella syndrome. Dev Med Child Neuro, 27, 721-729.

Frank, K. E., & Purnell, E. W. (1978). Subretinal neovascularization following rubella retinopathy. Am J Ophthalmol, 86, 462-466.

Gallagher, J. J., Beckman, P., & Cross, A. H. (1983). Families of handicapped children: Sources of stress and its amelioration. Except Child, 50, 10-19.

Gil, D. G. (1970). Violence against children: Physical and child abuse in the United States. Cambridge: Harvard University Press.

Goldfarb, L. A., Brotherson, M. J., Summers, J. A., & Turnbull, A. P. (1986). Meeting the challenge of disability or chronic illness—A family guide. Baltimore: Paul H. Brookes.

Green, E. M., & McIntosh, R. N. (1985). Food and nutrition skills of mentally retarded adults: assessment and needs. J Am Diet Assoc, 85, 611-613.

Haggerty, R. J. (1980). Life stress, illness and social supports. Dev Med Child Neuro, 22. 391-400.

Hassler, C. R. & Hostler, S. L. (1986). The adolescent interpretive interview. Unpublished manuscript.

Hostler, S. L., & Linden, P. G. (1981). Sexuality and the disabled adolescent. Presented at the Society for Adolescent Medicine, New Orleans.

Kurzweil, R. C. (1983). Reading machine for the blind. Med Electron, 14, 81-83.

Lobato, D. (1985). Brief report: Preschool siblings of handicapped children—Impact of peer support and training. J Aut Dev Dis, 15, 345-350.

Lowell, E. L. (1974). The construction of a table of distribution of time for various services and programs for the deaf-blind rubella children. In C. E. Sherrick (Ed.), 1980 is now: A conference on the future of deaf-blind children (pp. 15-16). John Tracy Clinic.

Lowell, E. L. (1974). Final recommendations for the conference. In C. E. Sherrick (Ed.), 1980 is now: A conference on the future of deaf-blind children (pp. 1-2). John Tracy Clinic.

Martin, E. W. (1985). Pediatrician's role in the care of disabled children. Peds Review, 6, 275-281.

Mattsson, A. (1972). Long-term physical illness in childhood: a challenge to psychosocial adaptation. Pediatrics, 50, 801-811.

Mellor, C. M. (1984). Aids for the '80s - What they are and what they do. New York: American Foundation for the Blind.

Menser, M. A., Dods, L., & Harley, J. D. A twenty-five year follow-up of congenital rubella. The Lancet, 2, 1347-1350.

Menser, M. A., Forest, J. M., Bransby, R. D., & Hudson, J. R. (1982). Long-term observation of diabetes and the congenital rubella syndrom in Australia. In G. Mimura, S. Baba, J. Goto V. Kobberling (Eds.), Clinicogenetic genesis of diabetes mellitus (pp. 221-225). Excerpta Medica.

Minuchin, S. (1974). Families and Family Therapy. Cambridge: Harvard University Press.

National Center on Child Abuse and Neglect. (1979). National analysis of official child abuse and neglect reporting, 1977 (p. 50). Department of Health and Human Services (Publication #OHDS 79-30232).

Newacheck, P. W., Budetti, P. P., & Halfon, N. (1986). Trends in Activity-limiting Chronic Conditions among Children, Am J Public Health, 76, 178-184.

Pans, Brown, & Vincent. (1986). Impact of having a child with disability on the family. Unpublished manuscript.

Peck, M. S. (1978). The Road Less Traveled (p. 316). New York: Simon and Schuster, Inc.

Preece, M. A., Kearney, P. J., & Marshall, W. C. (1977). Growth-hormone deficiency in rubella. Lancet, 2, 842-844.

Price-Bonham, S., & Addison, S. (1978). Families and mentally retarded children: emphasis on the father. Fam Coor, 3, 221-230.

Reid, K. (1983). The concept of interface related to services for handicapped families. Child: Care, Health and Development, 9, 109-118.

Reiger, N. I. (1974). Alternatives to hospitalizing developmentally handicapped children for care, treatment and education: Part 1. In C. E. Sherrick (Ed.), 1980 is now: A conference on the future of deaf-blind children (pp. 93-96). John Tracy Clinic.

Sandgrund, A., Gaines, R. W., & Green, A. H. (1974). Child abuse and mental retardation: A problem of cause and effect. Am J Men Def, 79, 327-330.

Schor, E. L., Smalky, K. A., & Neff, J. N. Primary care of previously institutionalized retarded children. Pediatrics, 67, 536-540.

Sever, J. L., South, M. A., & Shaver, K. A. Delayed Manifestations of Congenital Rubella. Rev Infect Dis, 7(51), S164-S169.

Shaver, K. (1983). Congenital rubella syndrome and diabetes: A study of genetic and epidemiologic risk factors. Unpublished doctoral dissertation. Richmond, VA: Virginia Commonwealth University.

Sicurella, V. (1977). Architecture for the visually impaired. J Impair Blind.

Simeonsson, R. J., & Simeonsson, N. E. (1981). Parenting handicapped children: Psychological perspectives. In J. Paul (Ed.), Understanding and Working with Parents of Children with Special Needs (pp. 51-88). New York: Holt, Rinehart and Winston.

Simon, N. Brighton Beach Memoirs. A play focusing on a family's response to adolescence, currently on Broadway.

Suelzle, M., & Keenan, V. (1981). Changes in family support networks over the life cycle of mentally retarded persons. Am J Ment Def, 86, 267-274.

Summers, J. A., Brotherson, J. J., & Turnbull, A. P. (1985). Coping strategies for families with disabled children. Adopted from Goldfarb, L., Brotherson, M. J., Summers, J. A. & Turnbull, A. P. Meeting the challenge of disability as chronic illness: A family guide. Baltimore: Paul Brookes.

Taft, L. T., Matthews, W. S., & Molnar, G. E. (1984). Pediatric Management of the Physically Handicapped Child (pp. 13-60). Year Book Medical Publishers, Inc.

Tarran, E. C. Parent's views of medical and social work services for families with young cerebral palsied children. Dev Med Child Neuro, 23, 173-182.

Taylor, S. J., Racino, J., Knoll, J., & Lutfiyya, Zana. (1986). The Nonrestrictive Environment: A Resource Manual on Community Integration for People with the Most Severe Disabilities, Field Test Version (pp. 1-141). Syracuse, NY: Syracuse University, Center on Human Policy.

Terkelsen, K. B. (1980). Toward a theory of the family life life cycle. In E. Carter and M. McGoldrick (Eds.), The Family Life Cycle: A Framework of Family Therapy (pp. 21-52). New York: Gardner Press.

Townsend, J. J., Baringer, J. R., Wolinsky, J. S., Malamud, W., Mednick, J. P., Panitch, H. S., Scott, R.A.T., Oshiro, L. S., & Cremer, N. E. (1975). Progressive rubella panencephalitis: Late onset after congenital rubella. New Eng J Med, 292, 990-993.

Turnbull, A. P., & Summers, J. S. (1985). From parent involvement to family support: Evolution to revolution (pp. 1-32). Presented at Down Syndrome State-of-the-Art Conference, Boston.

Turnbull, A. P., & Turnbull, R. (Eds.). (1986). Parents Speak Out. Columbus, Ohio: C. E. Merrill.

Vowles, M. (1981). Genetic counseling for handicapped school leavers. J Med Genetics, 18, 350-358.

Warren, N. S., Gallien, J. V., & Porter, G. (1982). Genetic counseling in a school for the deaf: A pilot program. Am Ann Deaf, 127, 401-4.

Waxham, M. N. & Wolinsky, J. S. (1984). Rubella virus and its effects on the central nervous system. Neurologic Clinics, 2, 367-385.

Wehman, P., & Hill, J. W. (1981). Competive employment for moderately and severely handicapped individuals. Except Child, 47, 338-345.

Weil, M. L., Habashi, H. H., Cremer, N. E., Oshiro, L. S., Lennette, E. H., & Carnay, L. (1975). Chronic progressive panencephalitis due to rubella virus simulating subacute sclerosing panencephalitis. New J Med, 292, 994-998.

Wheelis, Allen. (1973). How People Change. New York: Harper and Row.

Wolraich, M. L. (1982). Communication between physicians and parents of handicapped children. Except Child, 48, 324-329.

In Response to Sharon Hostler

A Medical Service Delivery System for Clients in New Jersey

Mary M. O'Donnell

It is an honor to be here at this conference and in such distinguished company.

I would like first to make some comments regarding Sharon's very inspiring talk and then tell you how we are developing a medical service delivery system for our community residence clients in New Jersey.

Sharon mentioned the conference, "1980 is Now." When it was completed and the proceedings published, it was hailed throughout the deaf-blind community as innovative and forward looking. It held the promise of a rosy future for all. We looked forward to a lifelong service delivery for those who are deaf-blind being in place by 1980. The conference was 12 years ago, folks. The promises should have been realities six years ago, and here we are at the crossroad, at 21 years old, at the time of transition! Many of us are finding that our children are transitioning into nothing!

I commend Helen Keller National Center for trying to coordinate through TAC (or correct the lack of) service for young adults who are deaf-blind. Now, we need a Catalyst-Coordinator or a mechanism to bring together key people from all corners of the U. S. to a place where they will have an opportunity to study the state of the art of service delivery to those who are deaf-blind. We need to hear what did not work for their clients or in their state; we need to hear of their successes, and the good people and the good systems in their local governments that facilitate success in a service delivery system that meets the needs of the citizen who is deaf-blind. We need to be inspired, encouraged, and rejuvenated by others who have the same dreams, goals, frustrations, and ideals for our people who have such unique needs.

Sharon mentioned that only two congenital rubella syndrome (CRS) cases were reported in 1985. That may very well be true. However, experience and a child-find program in New Jersey are constantly turning up new congenital deaf-blind cases caused by the drug culture. Also, the great strides in neonatal, postnatal care are increasing the survival rate for infants with severe problems. This must be true throughout the country. We in New Jersey are finding that preschool and school aged children who are deaf-blind are continuing to appear in surprisingly large numbers. This care, nurturing, education, and total service delivery for those who are deaf-blind of all ages is an ongoing, growing phenomenon. The need is not going to go away! Services are needed and, for the foreseeable future, will continue to be needed.

Health issues for this group will always be of primary concern. A multiplicity of problems must be treated and monitored on a continuing basis, and now history is showing us how important it is to monitor closely each of these folks, particularly those with CRS, to watch for glaucoma, diabetes, thyroid, coronary, and kidney problems which appear as they enter adulthood.

The all-inclusive wellness plan and adult care plans which Sharon has suggested offer a complete, well thought-out program. I hope we can find health providers with time and the interest in offering such programs. I hope we can find physicians who are willing to study the literature to stay current with the latest developments and treatment procedures. I hope, as new findings surface about CRS and other causes of deaf-blindness, there continues to be a forum for the exchange of information. Perhaps Helen Keller National Center will be the catalyst, perhaps some of our federal agencies should look toward acting as facilitators for a group such as those who are deaf-blind. But most of all, I hope that when we find the proper caretakers who are willing, knowledgeable, and able to care for the unique needs of the person who is deaf-blind, that we will also find the dollars to support the kind of wellness and adult health programs we need.

We will all be anxious to read Dr. Ann Turnbull's proceedings of the family conference referred to here. Although each family is different in so many ways, a common denominator is usually present in that the family wants each of its members to be safe, productive, and happy.

I commend Sharon for involving the family--particularly brothers and sisters--in the clients' lifetime plan. Families should be encouraged and offered nonthreatening opportunities for close contact with the disabled member without inconvenience or feeling of intrusion. All living arrangements should provide opportunities for family interaction.

In New Jersey, we are fortunate to have a well-developed human service delivery system. The Commission for the Blind, an offshoot of our Department of Human Services, has historically been the provider and facilitator of all service delivery to those who are deaf-blind in New Jersey. Fortunately, the Commission has developed a good working relationship with the State Department of Education and most school districts. Rehabilitation for citizens of New Jersey who are blind, including deaf-blind, is handled through the Commission for the Blind. The Department of Developmental Disabilities and Division of Youth and Family Service (also divisions of Department of Human Services) work cooperatively with the Commission to provide client services. I don't mean to suggest we live in a Utopian State! That's hardly the case. There are certainly flaws in the systems and, as always, the systems can only work as well as the people who implement them. We have some talented, dedicated, creative, and innovative people in New Jersey who have dedicated outstanding professional careers to the service of those who are deaf-blind; and we certainly have our share of "do-nothings" and "dead wood" always on hand to "mess up" a potentially good plan! But, at least we have an agency structure that can enhance service delivery when it's working well. This, unfortunately, is not the case in all states.

Over the years, we parents have had a rather loose-knit statewide parents group, sort of a support system, that sprung into action during times of crises but had no real structure. In the early 1980s, we parents of "the transition" group were becoming alarmed about the future as were some of our "caring" administrators at the Commission for the Blind. In late 1983, a grant was awarded to our nonprofit parent group, the New Jersey Association for the Deaf-Blind, by the Commission for the Blind. It provided operating expenses to hire an Executive Director and clerical help, and establish an office to facilitate delivery of services directly to those who are deaf-blind in our state, bypassing the great burden of bureaucracy which can so often hinder progress.

We've had our growing pains, and they will continue. However, one of our successes is my subject for today. We opened our first community residence for six young adult clients, 21-22 years of age, on February 10, 1986. The house was funded with, and support will continue to come from, Department of Developmental Disabilities resources. We selected the location, found the house, supervised renovations, dealt with all the inspectors, met all the code requirements, educated the town fathers, courted the neighbors, checked community resources--vocational, recreation, medical, leisure--developed staffing patterns and training procedures, purchased a van, furnishings, and recreation supplies. We developed our client selection criteria and, with the help of knowledgeable professionals, reviewed 14 clients presented from the Commission for the Blind and Department of Developmental Disabilities client registers to select our six for this first home.

The processes involved interviewing families, staff in schools clients attended, and using the resources of our own Commission for the Blind, Vocational Rehabilitation, Department of Developmental Disabilities, Helen Keller National Center, Technical Assistance Center, The Association for Persons with Severe Handicaps, United States Department of Education, in addition to the expert advice generously shared by those of you who have had experience in the development of residences. Also, our Executive Director had a valuable range of experience in residential development, in addition to excellent training skills which have been utilized in staff orientation and management.

After our clients were selected, but before they moved into their home, a detailed profile was developed for each. Medical histories were reviewed and updated with the previous program nursing staff; medical records were reviewed; and families were interviewed. Families were given the option to continue with doctors who had cared for their children or to use the team contacted by our agency. Parents made these choices based on location and convenience, and their wishes will be honored. Each client was required to have a physical before moving into the home.

Our general medical service contact is at one of the receiving hospitals of the location of the residence. This hospital has in place a well-established clinic with a team of specialists whose practices are devoted to treating the developmentally disabled. We hope and anticipate their cooperation in keeping abreast of and contributing to the literature and body of knowledge being developed about those who are deaf-blind. It is, of course, too soon to tell if this will happen. An initial screening and evaluation on each of the clients was completed at this clinic shortly after they moved into the home.

Four of our clients wear glasses, and three wear hearing aids. We contacted a local optician and hearing aid shop and both agreed to care for the appliances. They are ready for us if we need them.

A registered nurse of the Commision for the Blind staff has done inservice training for our house staff and will continue to do so periodically. This person will be "on call" for consultation. Local Fire Department and Rescue Squad personnel were contacted. They visited the house for inspection before occupancy, and since occupancy, have met the clients and conducted safety drills.

A dentist contacted through the New Jersey Association for Dentistry for the Handicapped has agreed to provide dental care for those clients who will not continue with their previous dentist.

Members of the Rubella Project at Roosevelt Hospital in New York City recently received ongoing grant money to continue monitoring and caring for their clients beyond

21 years. They have offered their services and will act as consultants to our staff. We are located about two hours from this facility. Dr. Zearing, whom many of you knew when he was with the Rubella Project, has also very kindly agreed to act as a medical consultant for our agency, and he is currently located only about 45 minutes from us.

The housemother is responsible for maintaining all health records. Menstrual cycles are charted—BMs are charted for those with problems. Appliances are checked and must be in good working order. (Menstrual and constipation problems, as well as nonworking appliances, are primary causes of discomfort and frustration among deaf-blind adolescents and youth. Most such individuals are unable to communicate the presence of these difficulties. Thus, acting out and inappropriate behaviors result. A major concern of parents, it is of utmost importance that all staff members are not only aware of these problems but take steps, on a daily basis, to prevent them.) Regular checkup appointments will be scheduled by the housemother, taking into consideration those medical problems for which the literature and our consultants feel this population may be in an "at risk" status. All staff have been alerted to be aware of signs or changes in behavior that may indicate medical problems.

One of our clients had a minor acting-out adjustment situation in the workplace. Prompt response and technical assistance from TASH have been most helpful in resolving this incidence.

We have been very conscious of the families and are encouraging active family participation. We will, of course, carry this philosophy through in all medically related areas for our clients. We tried to anticipate and plan for needed services before the clients moved into their home, using the profiles we had developed. Our goal was to be prepared to handle an emergency before it arose, to have a reasonable plan and resource available in anticipation of need. We will continue with this philosophy as experience teaches us where more areas of need may be.

I have one more area to address and hope you will be kind enough to bear with me. I must try to express my point of view! There has been and will be much talk at this conference of normalization, age-appropriate activities, and integrated work places.

Why do our young people who are disabled—deaf and blind—need to ask your permission to be different and unique? And why won't you, of all people, give them permission?

I submit here some food for your thought. Each of you in this room is out of step with normalization whether you have a high school diploma or a Ph.D. to prove your normalcy. Why? Because you are here! In today's materialistic world where the dollar and what it can buy (self-indulgence) where the yuppie and "ME" cultures are popular, you are giving your talents, energies, and time to develop a better quality of life for those less able than yourselves. You have permission to be different and unique, to associate and work with your peers, and choose your recreation according to your likes.

At some point you left your parents' home as many of our children are doing. Did you expect necessarily to live and work within a few miles of your parents' home? Did you choose your line of work with a quota system in mind? "I'll be the white Catholic, female, Irish descent, middle-income background, B.A. degree, blue-eyed, blonde in your integrated workplace!" Was this your parent's dream for you? Is it yours for your children?

Most likely, you live close to where you work. You work at something you enjoy doing, with people who have interests and skills compatible with yours. You choose your friends because they're like you; you have common interests; you can communicate well with each other.

If you have a serious medical problem and you have a reasonable choice, you will live where care is accessible. If necessary, you will consider the quality and need for transportation when choosing your residence. Has anyone told you lately you can't sit on the backyard swing, on the park swing, or go on the amusements at the fair because these activities are not age-appropriate?

When planning for our children who often cannot make their own decisions, let's consider them each different and unique! Consider their likes, dislikes, and comfort; their environmental and communication needs; what activities they enjoy for recreation opportunities; how they wish to live, work, and recreate in the company of their peers. Our children are different and unique; please respect their differences and uniqueness, and cater to them!

In Response to Sharon L. Hostler

Principles and Practices of Community Integration
for Persons with Severe and Profound Disabilities

Hank A. Bersani, Jr.

I want today to speak about the issue of social change and how we have come to have newer, better services for people with severe, profound, and multiple disabilities. I also want to give a template for today's discussion and ask people to think about social change in the past as happening in three related spheres: the sphere of ideology, the sphere of practice, and the sphere of legal initiative. First, I want to explain what each of these means.

Three Spheres of Social Change

Ideology. If we use as an example the issue of integrated education for children with severe handicaps, we see that we began with a well-defined ideology. We knew that we wanted to find ways for children without handicaps and children with handicaps to go to school together. Over the years, that ideology became more and more well articulated. We said it is desirable for all children to go to school together in truly integrated settings, without regard to their labels, abilities, or disabilities.

Practice. Simultaneous to the development of that ideology, we made improvements in educational practice to the point that we were able to teach children we had previously thought could not be taught, and to teach children in integrated settings whom we previously thought required segregated settings. So we experienced an increase in sophistication in terms of the state of the art of integrated education.

Legal initiative. The third change was in the legal sphere. The passage of Public Law 94-142 gave a legal mandate for the education of all handicapped children. Thus we had the ideology that it was desirable for all children to be educated together, the practical skills to be successful, and the legal mandate, which required integration and made some money available to encourage that all children be educated together. These three together resulted in major social change.

When we talk about social services, especially residential services, for people with severe handicaps, we are at this point still lacking a legal mandate. We don't have a residential equivalent of P.L. 94-142, but a great deal has happened in terms of ideology. I also wish to discuss the public policy issues that I think point the way for a legal mandate.

The Story of Amy and Jimmy

I want to tell you the stories of two children whom we met in the research project that I am affiliated with. We call these children Amy and Jimmy. Amy is a girl, and Jimmy is a boy; otherwise they have a lot in common. Both are eight years old. They both have hydrocephaly and a multitude of associated problems, including blindness, and seizures. Both take nutrition by g-tubes, and are susceptible to choking, infection, bed sores, and sudden drops in body temperature or hypothermia. Fortunately for Amy and Jimmy, they happen to live in states where people are committed to serving children with severe disabilities in the community. Jimmy lives with five other children in a Medicaid-certified group home just outside Gibson Landing, Michigan, and Amy lives with her foster parents, Mr. and Mrs. Parker, in Lincoln, Nebraska.

We have a several-page description of how the children's lives now go (Taylor, Racino, Knoll, & Lutfiyya, 1986). What becomes very clear is that, first of all, there was the supportive ideology. Michigan and Nebraska are states in which people are committed to serving children with severe disabilities in the community. Second, these children are receiving clinical services, the "hands-on" intervention, that make it possible for them to live in a community whereas, just a few years ago, conditions like hydrocephaly, hypothermia, blindness, seizures, and certainly the use of gastric tubes would be clear indicators of an inability to live in a community. Here we see strides in both practice and ideology, and are seeing now the development of policy statements that will lead to, I think, a legal foundation for greater services. As we have learned over the past fifteen years in developmental disabilities, there is a common link of several basic principles that are not disability-specific. I believe that these principles apply equally to deaf-blindness as well as severe and profound mental retardation, and people called "medically fragile." In short, these principles apply to all of the people we call the "most difficult to serve."

The Ideology of Integration

The two projects that I am affiliated with through the Syracuse University Center on Human Policy--one project called the Community Integration Project, and the second called the Research and Training Center on Community Integration, of which I am the Director--have jointly developed a series of policy statements about integrated community living, and I want to share those with you now. They are, for the most part, self-explanatory.

1. People with developmental disabilities, including those with the most severe disabilities, should be served in their home communities.

The development of this chapter was supported through Contract No. G0085C03503 between the Center on Human Policy, Syracuse University, and the National Institute on Handicapped Research, U. S. Department of Education. The opinions expressed herein do not necessarily represent those of the U. S. Department of Education and no endorsement should be inferred.

2. Community living arrangements should be on a family scale and should be located in residential neighborhoods.
3. Services should support people in typical homes, jobs, and community environments.
4. Services should foster the development of practical life skills.
5. Parents, as well as those who have the disabilities, should be involved in the design, operation and monitoring of services.

These policy statements indicate a change from the old kind of model of forming group homes for eight or twelve or fifteen people for everybody who comes down the line. People don't come in cases of 24, or in half cases of 12, or even 6-packs. People come as families and as individuals as people who have friends, and as people who have their own individual needs. If we are going to begin to devise a service system for all people with all types of severe disabilities, that service system needs to focus on the concept of a home, particularly with children, but even with adults. People should be supported whenever possible in their own natural homes. If the natural family (sometimes called the biological family) cannot or is not willing to keep that person at home, even with substantial supports, then we need to move on to an adoptive environment. Only if adoption is clearly out of the picture (and we are finding more and more that adoption is reasonable for people who were previously called unadoptable), only then will we look at foster care for a child. Only after we have explored supporting the family—an adoptive family or a foster family—would we then begin to think about other settings such as group settings. In day-to-day practice, we may need to compromise, but our ideology must be clear: families first.

Several systems around the country are saying no to group-based care for children, even for children with the most severe disabilities. The Macomb-Oakland region north of Detroit serves a population base of 3 million people and, as of today, has only seventeen children in the entire population base who are living in other than family settings—five children in one group home, ten children in a transitional ICF/MR, and two additional children currently in the regional center. By Christmas 1986, they plan to have all of those children into foster homes, adoptive homes, or biological homes.

As a result of the experience in systems like Macomb-Oakland, we are rethinking the need for a so-called residential continuum. We have talked for too long about the need for a continuum of buildings such as large group homes, small group homes, specialized group homes for people with behavior problems, specialized group homes for people with medical needs. We have focused on buildings. We have had what I would like to call an "edifice complex," focusing too much on the buildings and too little on supports. We need to realize from lessons learned over the past fifteen years that buildings are not services. We do not need a continuum of buildings; we do need an array of services. If we focus too much on buildings we get into a dilemma that Seymour Sarason has written about (1972) where the building becomes a distraction or a trap. We talk more about my building and less about the service.

As we direct our attention to services, we must be aware of what I call the "self-satisfaction trap." There is great pressure in the field of severe disabilities to identify "model" programs and then, if you will, anoint them as the service we should all seek to emulate. There are at least two problems in identifying model programs. The first problem is that so-called model programs are never as good as we say they are or will be. Our old ideas pale so by comparison that we over sell the new model.

The second problem with the self-satisfaction of "models" is resistance to change. If we say that we are a "model" program, then there is no need for us to change. Then we become what I call "a failing success," and in 15 years, the "model" is still in the same place with fifteen-year-old technology, fifteen-year-old innovation, fifteen-year-old service models that are no longer innovative, and are no longer "model," and often no longer even adequate.

As I've visited a variety of school programs as well as residential programs, I have kept a list of what I called "lessons learned" over the years, things that we maybe didn't do so well in the past, or things that have become obvious as we had more experience with integration.

Lessons Learned

Good teachers can teach anyone, and bad teachers should not teach at all. We don't need to have two groups of teachers—special education teachers and regular education teachers. The ability of a teacher to cope with differences is intrinsic to being a good teacher, and teachers who lack that ability, teachers who cannot cope with differences in the classroom, cannot be accepted as a reason for segregating children. Rather than seeking out segregated settings because teachers cannot cope with differences, we need to seek out teachers who can cope with those differences.

There is no aspect of so-called regular education that cannot benefit all students. Everyone can benefit from being in a regular classroom with a variety of students. There is not just one middle group that benefits from regular education with those who are handicapped needing one type of special education and those who have the other terrible label, "gifted and talented," needing another type. Students will learn best together.

There is no aspect of so-called "special education" that cannot be practiced by any good teacher. The principles of individualization, program planning, writing IEPs, doing a task analysis, high repetition, or whatever it is that constitutes special education are not magic. Any good teacher can master these techniques.

We have focused in the past entirely too much attention on independence as a goal. What we have learned recently is that independence is really not an appropriate goal for anyone; all people must learn to be interdependent. None of us in our own lives are truly independent; we are all interdependent. This misplaced emphasis on independence can eat up a great deal of concern and instructional time. While being independent has its place, we are dealing with people who will for the rest of their lives need to learn to be interdependent.

One's ability to function interdependently is not related directly to one's ability to function independently. That is, we can't increase someone's ability to be interdependent by giving them more personal independence skills; some people will do very well at being interdependent with fewer independence skills. As they gain skills of independence, those skills may not help their ability to be interdependent at all; in fact, they may get in the way. If we focus too much on independence, we may fail to give a person opportunities to function interdependently.

Educational settings need to be truly integrated, not just "mainstreamed." To be integrated means to become a part of, to be made whole. We no longer can justify segregated schools, or even segregated classes based on educational differences or medical differences. Educational settings can be truly integrated in ways that benefit all the students involved.

Heterogeneity is preferable to homogeneity. Again, we have in the past tried to seek more and more homogeneous settings where we would put everybody with behavior disorders in one program so that we could specialize the staff. But we found that what used to be called behavior-shaping units are now in some places called behavior-sharing units because everybody begins to share their inappropriate behaviors. The homogeneous grouping worked against us. Homogeneous grouping has clearly presented problems in programming for people labeled autistic. We take a group of children who don't make eye contact, don't relate well, don't initiate friendships, and put them in a roomful of other students who don't make eye contact, don't make friends well, and don't initiate contacts, and after a year we say, "My goodness what a surprise! This person still doesn't make eye contact, doesn't initiate contacts, and doesn't form relationships." That homogeneous grouping clearly works against them, and it will work against students grouped on the basis of their deaf-blindness as well. We need to achieve a level of heterogeneity, or what Lou Brown has called "natural proportions."

106

This doesn't mean mixing only people with various disabilities. Heterogeneity should include large numbers of people who have no disabilities and a small, natural proportion of those with other disabilities, so that we see the full range and spectrum of life. Homogeneity results in an unnatural or excessive congregation of people with certain types of needs. Then those needs become blown out of proportion and become overwhelming.

Social integration is more important than physical integration. Many programs these days are focusing on getting people physically integrated. Our residences are located in regular neighborhoods. Our classrooms are located in a regular school. We go out to the community on a regular basis, and that is good. That kind of physical integration is a necessary step to social integration. But the only reason physical integration is worth doing is if it some day leads to social integration, such as being involved with people, going to school with other students, making friends, not just being located in a residential neighborhood. So we need to think more about social integration beyond physical integration.

Acceptance cannot precede integration. There is a lot of talk these days saying that we'll mainstream the schools more when the school children are ready, when they are more accepting. Or we'll put a group home in the neighborhood when the neighbors are ready, when they are more accepting. Social acceptance is an <u>outcome</u> of integration, it is not a <u>requirement</u> for it. We cannot go into segregated schools full of students who are labeled normal, armed with puppets and blindfold walk experiences, and expect them to develop social acceptance. Acceptance comes from personal experience with peers with disabilities.

Friends are more important than volunteers. Too many programs today attempt mainstreaming by setting up so-called special friends and buddy systems, where nonhandicapped children are "assigned" to a handicapped peer. In some programs, members of a youth group earn points for "logging" a specific number of hours with students with special needs. The overriding human need is for long-term, freely given, personal relationships. These are not necessarily generated by volunteer projects and helper-helpee relationships. True friendships cannot be legislated, programmed, or trained. They can only be nurtured, and that takes time.

Three Decision Rules

Promoting community integration is a complex procedure. We could list about a dozen rules for promoting the physical and social integration of people with profound disabilities into society. In the context of today's discussion, I want to offer three questions that I believe will focus our attention on the essentials of integration.

Is the community involved? Seymour Sarason (1972), who writes extensively about creating community-based settings, said, "a program which purports to be community oriented is not consistent with its purpose if it accepts cases in ways which absolve the community of continuing, concrete responsibility" (p. 172). That is, if we say that we are a community-based program, we can't then assume full responsibility ourselves for everything that those people need. We have a problem in the developmental disabilities field of seeking out developmental disability specialist physicians and developmental disability specialist psychologists and dentists and home visitation nurses, to the point that we relieve the rest of the community of any need for ongoing continuous concrete involvement in our program with our people. I've been calling this a "responsibility trap." The more things that we assume responsibility for as service providers, the more responsibility we absolve the community from having. Then we are surprised that the community doesn't know about people with special needs.

I recently read a magazine article in which the author was reflecting on a mistake (from his point of view), that the gay community in California had made around the issue of AIDS. They had developed a history of going only to so-called "Gay Physicians," physicians who were not necessarily gay themselves, but who specialized in dealing with gay men, and then as the AIDS epidemic grew, they stayed only with those physicians, so that they had in fact _absolved_ the rest of the medical community from knowing about people who were gay in general or about AIDS in particular. I was stunned by the fact that this man realized the limits of this approach with just two or three years experience around AIDS. It is something that we have been practicing for twenty years in mental retardation and developmental disabilities, and many places still have not yet realized that if we claim to be a community-based program, we need to be careful not to absolve the community of ongoing involvement with our programs and with our people.

Does it promote quality of life? Mark Gold made a series of videotapes portraying people. In the last videotape he made before he died, Mark dealt with the issues of quality of life, and talked about the things that are important to all of us, whether handicapped or not. He talked about privacy, meaning not just modesty or being able to close the bathroom door, but also having time alone. If you live in groups of 6 or 8, with staff coming and going in three shifts, you experience very little privacy, little or no time to yourself. Modesty is also difficult to manage with men and women staff working with men and women who need help bathing, and are living in group of 6 or 8 or 12 or 15 or more. Privacy is clearly one of the ways in which we measure the quality of our own lives, and it should be a quality marker in the lives of those we serve.

The second quality indicator that Mark Gold mentioned was that of choice. Do people have choices? He points out that when you talk to service providers, particularly residential providers, they say something very interesting. They say, "Oh yes, we let them choose." Gold says that you can't "let" somebody choose. It doesn't work that way. That by saying that you "let" people do it, it is not really a matter of choice. Choice has to be something that people _have_, not something they are _allowed_. He goes on to talk about the merits of dignity, status, and respect, things that we all want for ourselves. We want to have a certain dignity, status, and to be treated with respect. These are difficult traits to afford people whom we think of as having a set of syndromes, or as being clients, or as being severely handicapped.

He also talks a bit about the importance of reciprocity of relationships. I can relate to this very well because it is something that I found in a study I did of staff in community residences for adults with mental retardation. I was struck by the contrast between the lives of the staff and the lives of the residents. I asked staff about what were the satisfactions that helped them get through the bad times in working in residences. They answered by talking about a person who was previously reluctant to share and wouldn't open up, or wouldn't engage in a personal relationship with a staff member. They would tell a story to the effect that one day the person was bothered, and said "no," they didn't want to talk about it. So the staff member said, "Well, I may not be able to help you but I would be very willing to at least discuss it with you. I wish you would open up, and at least share with me, and tell me what it is that's bothering you." And then, one day, the resident did in fact open up and share. Maybe the staff member was able to fix the problem, maybe they couldn't, but they felt good knowing that someone had trusted them enough to share and tell them what was on their mind. That was what staff said gave them satisfaction, a sense of self-worth.

We must ask ourselves how many occasions have there been in this setting in which the _resident_ has offered to console a _staff_ member. Does the staff member accord that same dignity to the residents? As a staff member, I was always trained to say "no, you know we are here to work on your problems, not on mine." We, in fact, systematically have denied to others that very satisfaction we find so strong for ourselves. The issue is not whether they are in any position to help us with our problems. Very often we can't help the people who share with us. The issue is that by sharing our problems with somebody else, we afford them equal status, dignity, and respect through that reciprocal relationship.

The last thing that Gold talks about in terms of quality of life is in the context of rules. Any family or household has rules, just like any program or facility or residence.

The true differences are in who makes the rules, and what are the underlying values of the rules. In a program, the rules are made by the few (the staff) for the many (the people who actually live there), as opposed to a household in which the rules are appropriately made by all the people who live there, instead of by outsiders who don't live there. The underlying values in a family or household could be that we want to make this a good place to live with opportunities for sharing, and taking into account everybody's concerns. The rules in a group home or in a facility generally don't have the same level of quality. The rules tend to focus on what will help things run efficiently, or what is good for the staff, or what is good for the program, or what is required by funding—a very different origin for those rules. When we think about what would be a quality program, we need to direct ourselves to the issues of privacy, choice, dignity, status and respect, reciprocity of relationships, and the rules and where they come from and whom they affect.

What is the potential for harm? The last question comes from Ira Glasser of the ACLU (1978). He is not an expert in services, per se, but is someone who has given a lot of thought to how to tell what is good when you see it and what is not so good. In a chapter he wrote called "Prisoners of Benevolence, Power vs. Liberty in the Welfare State," he talks about people and liberty. The words he uses are "seduced and ravaged by good intentions." We say that we are going to help people, but, in fact, we destroy their liberty and detract from their lives. He proposes what he calls a doctrine of least harm. Instead of looking at programs that are designed to help people and evaluating them on the basis of how much good they might do, he says we need to look at them for their potential to do harm, and that we should adopt those programs that seem less likely to make things worse. He maintains that if we had that point of view, we would never have had institutionalized atrocities like those at Willowbrook. The doctrine of least harm will be familiar to folks with medical backgrounds as the doctrine of "at least do no harm." We clearly established institutions in the guise of trying to help people. We have done them more harm by segregating and isolating and doing things that enhance their differences rather than enhancing their humanness and giving them more opportunities.

If there is anything to be learned from the last ten or fifteen years in terms of services to people with severe disabilities, this is it. If we could just stop doing harm we would be well on our way to doing good.

References

Glasser, R. (1978). Prisoners of benevolence: Power versus liberty in the welfare state. In W. Gaglin, I. Glasser, S. Marcus, & D. Rothman (Eds.), Doing good: The limits of benevolence. New York: Pantheon Books.

Sarason, S. (1972). The creation of settings and the future societies. San Francisco: Jossey-Bass Inc.

Taylor, S., Racino, J., Knoll, J., & Lutfiyya, Z. (1986). The nonrestrictive environment: A resource manual on community intergration for people with the most severe disabilities. Syracuse University, Center on Human Policy.

Report of the Working Group on Health/Psychosocial Issues and Services

Group Members

Joann Boughman   William Jones
Richard Bunner   Virginia Lapham
Patricia Fleming   Mary O'Donnell
Sharon Hostler

Report prepared by Virginia Lapham and Joann Boughman

Introduction

This report addresses the transitional health and psychosocial needs of the estimated 2,000-4,000 youth and young adults with both hearing and visual impairments. Legally defined as "deaf-blind," most of these youth, in particular those with congenital rubella syndrome, have additional handicaps affecting their communication, ambulation, and cognitive development, which also places them in the larger category of severely and profoundly handicapped. Recognizing the paucity of appropriate services for deaf-blind and profoundly handicapped youth and adults, it is urgent that a comprehensive physical and psychosocial health care system be developed to meet the transitional needs of this vulnerable population.

Of primary importance is the recognition of the individual and diverse needs of the individuals with profound/muliple handicaps and deafness-blindness. It is essential to understand the need for flexibility of options in health care, and imperative to acknowledge the fundamental right of access to comprehensive and appropriate care for physical and psychosocial health needs.

Service Approach

The ultimate goal of a comprehensive health care system is the utilization of the interdisciplinary health care team in providing an adult health care plan to

1. develop assessment mechanisms;
2. implement comprehensive individual care plans;
3. develop a case mangement system to access services, follow through, keep records of current health needs;
4. disseminate current information to all providers in the system as appropriate.

The main objective in the establishment of a comprehensive health care system for profoundly/multiply handicapped deaf-blind is the coordination and integration of services addressing both medical and psychosocial aspects of health.

Issues and Considerations

For ease in addressing responsibilities and issues, this report is separated into five "levels" of care provision: individuals (patients, cases, or clients); families; groups (group homes, community living situations); health care providers; and agencies. Although some themes are repetitive, the specific issues and possible actions and responses vary among the levels.

I. Individuals

A. Responsibilities. The development of a comprehensive health care system for profoundly/multiply handicapped deaf-blind youth requires better definition of the needs of this very special population, with particular emphasis on the integration of services for physical and psychosocial aspects of health.

B. Issues.

1. Individual differences in abilities and needs must be clearly recognized.
2. The necessity to address age-appropriate health care is imperative to adequate care.
3. Individual rights and privileges including privacy and safety must be addressed.
4. Access to effective case management services (ombudsman) is necessary to ensure that quality care and rights are being honored.

II. Families

A. Responsibilities. The family unit has been defined as a multigenerational group of people who transmit values and share love and loyalty. While the usual family group may include immediate biological or adopted relatives (parents, siblings) or extended families, similar needs and issues are common to other units which are primarily responsible for the care (physical and emotional) of these multiply handicapped persons. Such relationships may include surrogate families, or group care providers who are primarily responsible for the immediate and continual care of these individuals.

B. Issues. Several issues are of primary importance to "family members" to satisfy their own needs as they relate to and care for multiply handicapped youth or young adults.

1. The diversity of opinions and individual needs within and among "families" must be recognized and addressed.
2. The needs and desires of the "family" must be considered in service development.
3. Financial issues and constraints should be recognized.
4. Values and moral systems of the "family" should be respected, especially when addressing sensitive issues such as sexuality.

5. Issues of transition that must be recognized and directly addressed include separation from family or other caregivers, and development of confidence and trust in newly responsible persons, community resources, and quality assurance.

III. Groups (Alternative Living Arrangements, Community-based Services)

A. Responsibilities. The development of homes and community-based services facilitate the very important development of normalization and integration into the community. Such units also address the problems of societal acceptance and interpersonal relationships. Although often not clearly recognized, the interdependence among peers and their caretakers and immediate community evolves from these settings. It is the responsibility of this group of caretakers to identify and understand the impact of their unit on the community in which they reside.

B. Issues. Although many similarities exist between "groups" and families, additional issues are of utmost importance in the development of an adequate group care system. The necessary qualifications and competency must be characterized, since these caretakers will be providers outside the usual health care system. The mechanisms for funding and decisions about financial responsibility must be clarified.

IV. Direct Health Care Providers

A. Responsibilities. The health care professionals who are participating in provision of care to this population are responsible for acquiring the training and expertise to understand and provide adequate and comprehensive health care to these individuals. The professionals must develop rapport with the patients and their caretakers, as well as recognize the need for referral and long-term follow-up. Expert professionals should serve as consultants to the systems and agencies in preparing guidelines, developing models, and monitoring progress.

B. Issues. Some issues are similar to those raised with caretakers, including

1. identification of basic qualifications and skills including communication as well as medical expertise,
2. understanding of the impact of issues important to the family including protection, privacy, sexuality, and the rights of individuals.

Other issues include

3. the recognition of potential biases in the health care system, and honest attempts to provide truly comprehensive long-term as well as acute health care;
4. knowledge of communication modes, appliances, and interpreter services, and acceptance and willingness to interact openly with patients and family members;
5. up-to-date information regarding medical issues, and information on a case by case basis readily shared with all service providers of the individual;
6. recognition that availability and funding of services and medical resources is not uniform;
7. recognition of the full range of health services (i.e. nutrition, physical therapy, etc.) beyond primary and referral physician care.

V. Agencies

A. Responsibilities. Local, state and federal agencies are responsible for development of policies and regulations regarding service delivery for profoundly/multiply handicapped deaf-blind persons. In addition, these agencies are also responsible for guidelines for training programs. Recognition of available resources, identification of funding sources, and provision of funding through several mechanisms are all the responsibility of governmental agencies.

B. Issues. In addition to the issues related to provision of comprehensive care to individuals and families, agencies must deal with the issues of limitations and barriers created by laws and mandated policies. Such barriers include age restrictions to service programs and mandated services (e.g., in most states restricted to under age 21) and limitations in payment for services due to definitions of handicaps and limitations of served populations.

Recommendations

This section is organized into the same categories as the issues and considerations sections: Individuals, Families, Groups, Health Care Providers, and Agencies. In addition, a summary recommendation section is included.

Individuals

1. Capitalization on the period of transition for planning and needs assessment for adult life (see Hostler).
2. Development of a health assessment that includes review of health documents, a current health profile, and review of symptoms and concerns of caretakers. A complete adult physical examination should be a part of the assessment. This assessment plan should be initiated prior to transition (e.g., age 18) to prepare adequately for adult health care.
3. Implementation of a comprehensive health care plan dictates special attention to the following areas:
   a. promotion of wellness;
   b. identification and diagnosis of late onset sequelae of deaf-blindness syndromes including
      (1) cardiovascular complications,
      (2) endocrinopathies (e.g., diabetes, thyroid),
      (3) autoimmune disorders,
      (4) neurological abnormalities,
      (5) behavior disorders;
   c. transition from pediatric to adult health care issues such as
      (1) sexual function/dysfunction,
      (2) secondary sexual development.
4. Design of a checklist format of key areas of health assessment and care that could be utilized uniformly by all health and service providers to ensure addressing all critical health issues.
5. Design of an adult care plan including management of current health problems, intercurrent care, and critical care.
6. Development of more complete applications of scientific/technological advancements as appreciation grows regarding the importance of these devices.

Family

1. Development of assessment protocols (for families) that clearly address the family's needs, desires, and stresses that relate to the care of profoundly, multiply handicapped deaf-blind persons, along with identification of strengths and weaknesses in the family unit.
2. Identification and development of support services for families by
   a. establishing peer support and education groups for parents and siblings;
   b. enhancing and coordinating professional mental health services;
   c. identifying and expanding state agency and voluntary services including
      (1) surrogate families,
      (2) intervener programs (e.g., Canadian Model),
      (3) surrogate siblings and grandparents,

(4) paid companions

(5) community trusts.

3. Identification and improvement of funding resources for family units caring for these adults.

4. Location and dissemination of new information and data regarding family studies to professionals, agencies, and families in a timely fashion.

5. Development of a case management link for individual and family services.

Groups (Alternative Living Arrangements, Community-based Services)

1. Model programs (such as Seattle and New Jersey) should be identified, and the information regarding their development made freely available through as many sources as possible (education, Maternal and Child Health, University Affiliated Facility, Helen Keller National Center, Administration for Developmental Disabilities, Office of Special Education and Rehabilitation Services, etc.).

2. Potential funding sources should be identified and working financial models made available.

3. Research into innovative partnerships with private and philanthropic agencies should be encouraged.

4. Definition and development of a "case manager" model system should be pursued in the following ways:

   a. federal funding of a conference for sharing of models,

   b. provision of funding for demonstration projects of various models

   c. sharing of current developments through a network of "case manager" professionals,

   d. definition of the case managers as coordinators of diverse physical and mental health care services,

   e. development of evaluation and monitoring of quality assurance measures for these professionals.

5. Funding should be made of studies of the advantages and disadvantages in rural versus urban settings for such facilities.

6. Creative mechanisms should be developed for coordination and transport of mobile health services to these facilities to enhance the comprehensive care of clients.

7. Mechanisms of leadership and organization of home health care teams and all medical support systems, including policies and procedures, should be developed.

8. Barrier removal and enhancement of technology should be encouraged to improve physical and psychosocial health.

Direct Health Care Providers

1. Identification of experts and encouragement of the dissemination of their new research findings to a broad audience.

2. Encouragement (and funding) of health care providers to provide adequate training to new professionals, such as through the University Affiliated Facility (UAF) network.

3. Development of continuing education programs for health care providers which focus on the problems of the population in question.

4. Consideration of medical and psychological health research projects focusing on this population as an immediate priority for funding through federal resources.

5. Development of new relationships should be developed with professionals from other disciplines (e.g. environmental and recreational engineers) to enhance the development of innovative devices for use by these clients.

6. Development of regionalized teams of health professionals representing several medical disciplines because the health care needs of this population are so complex. This model should permit more complete health care provision, while absolving individual primary health care providers from performing all aspects of total health care.

7. Identification of adult onset problems associated with syndromes causing multiple handicaps in deaf-blind persons and dissemination of this information to appropriate specialists to enhance health care.

Agency

1. At the national level and with federal support, policy should be developed which mandates the collection of badly needed information regarding the adult health care needs of the population in question.
2. With the advice of experts representing a broad range of subspecialities, guidelines for comprehensive assessment protocols should be established and published from the federal system.
3. Guidelines for staff qualifications for group home personnel and case managers should be developed and made readily accessible.
4. Special efforts at federal and state levels should be made to recognize and eliminate systemic problems in funding services such as age limitations and geographic barriers (e.g. state lines). Models which utilize MCH funds for special programs (e.g. genetics) may be utilized.
5. Networks of health care providers across the country should be established for the full and timely sharing of both effective and ineffective methods for providing comprehensive services.
6. Agencies with special funding and expertise should be utilized to their fullest capacities including UAF's, ADD, TAC, MCH, HKNC. Special projects of high priority should include
   a. provision of specialized training for providers including case managers by HKNC;
   b. support for an interdisciplinary conference by MCH to discuss available information and health issues of the adults who are multiply handicapped with deaf-blindness and dissemination of gathered information;
   c. sponsorship of a conference on development of a workable care (or case) manager system that functions in conjunction with, but outside the aegis of, funding agencies to avoid conflict of interest;
   d. continued support and expansion of HKNC as a technical assistance center for transition adult multiply handicapped deaf-blind persons; and
   e. utilization of HKNC for repository and clearing house for dissemination of state of the art information on services for this population.

A Summary of the Above Recommendations

1. To enhance the comprehensive nature of services there should be sharing of responsibilities among agencies at federal, state, and local levels for program development and fiscal responsibility.
   a. focus should be placed on an interagency collaborative model at the federal level among OSERS, MCH, and ADD to promote joint projects and gather information;
   b. new methods for collaboration between public and private sectors should be sought.
2. New models should be developed for mechanisms of total case management for individuals and their families.
3. Competency of all providers should be assessed, with emphasis on their total acceptance of those who are deaf-blind and multiply handicapped. Training should be provided and salaries offered that promote long-term employment.
4. Technology and knowledge, now shared on an ad hoc basis should be more universally applied with more forceful delivery methods and implementation of strategies:
   a. HKNC should be funded to continue and expand services including repository for information and training of providers;

b. UAFs should take active role in research and training of this population;

c. MCH, OSERS, and ADD should continue collaborative leadership role in policy and support of comprehensive services and act as a role model for state and local interagency cooperation.

SECTION IV: RECREATION AND LEISURE

Recreation and Leisure: Practices in Educational Programs
Which Hold Promise for Adult Service Models

Lori Goetz

Introduction

The current state of the art in recreation and leisure programs and services for persons with severe multiple disabilities has been comprehensively reviewed by several authors (Compton, Burrows, & Witt, 1979: Putnam, Werder, & Schleien, 1985; Voeltz, Wuerch & Wilcox, 1982; Wehman & Schleien, 1981). Based upon my own background, the focus of this paper will be upon what we know to be "model indicators" for recreation and leisure programming in educational contexts with school-aged individuals who have severe and profound disabilities including dual sensory impairments. With those indicators identified, I will review services currently available to young adults and their families in transition, and offer some initial suggestions on how we might integrate knowledge gained from school-based programs with current programs provided by community-based service agencies. It is hoped that these suggestions will serve as a starting point for our small group discussions.

Definitions: What Is Leisure? What Is Recreation?

The dictionary defines leisure as "freedom from time-consuming duties or activities," and recreation as "refreshment of the mind or body after labor through diverting activity." Neither definition provides much concrete information to agencies and/or individuals seeking to improve recreation and leisure services for a specific group of people. While a precise definition remains elusive, several components of recreation and leisure are important to note:

Discretionary time (Putnam et al., 1985; Voeltz et al., 1982). Leisure and recreation take place when an individual is _not_ doing the other activities, duties, and responsibilities that are required of him (usually by someone else). For school-age students, leisure takes place before, after, or between required activities that occur at home, at school, or in the community. For transition-aged young adults, leisure and recreation take place before, after, or between required activities in the workplace, at home, and in the community. This variability in the _times_ (and therefore also in the _places_) when leisure skills are needed and used means that an individual's leisure and recreational skill needs affect all other domains and environments in which she participates. (Recreation may take place during a break at work, after dinner at home, and in a community recreation center on the weekend.)

Variable location. As mentioned above, variable locations are another component of the recreation leisure domain. Persons recreate in all sorts of different places: there is nothing about leisure and recreation that restricts it to specified "leisure" environments. However, leisure-specific environments also exist, including park and recreation agencies (municipal recreation centers), community education agencies, and voluntary clubs (YMCA), with services available on both an episodic and sporadic basis. Thus, both when and where people recreate is based on highly individual factors.

I would like to thank both Dr. Terry Dolan and Barbara Ryan for their thoughtful commentaries and add that I very much agree with their remarks. Dr. Dolan's comment concerning the importance of communication skills for deaf-blind individuals is an excellent one. I think, in relation to making and expressing choices, we need especially to remember that persons with dual sensory impairments may express their preferences in ways which are nonconventional, idiosyncratic, and not reflective of standard language systems or communicative forms of behavior (see Donellan, Mirenda, Mesaras, Fassbender, 1984). Failure to use a conventional form to express choice should not result in denial (intentional or unintentional) of an expressed leisure preference; service providers must therefore possess skills that go beyond only recreation and leisure to understanding and utilizing the communication system that any person uses.

Personal choice (Bull, 1972; Murphy, 1981; Voeltz et al., 1982). Recreation and leisure activities provide ideal opportunities for people to exercise choice and personal preferences. A leisure activity is defined in part by the fact that it is something an individual chooses to do, versus something that an individual is required to do. Indeed, some investigators have suggested that the omission of choice in the participation process may prevent individuals from genuine leisure experiences (Datillo & Barnett, 1985). Certainly, if one indicator of quality of life is the number of choices available to an individual, then both the skills and the opportunities needed to exercise meaningful choices are essential components of recreation and leisure.

Variability in the time and place when recreation is experienced, combined with the role of personal preference and choice in leisure results in several unique implications for service delivery. The first has to do with the types of recreation and leisure skill needs that individual young adults in transition and their families might have. If an individual is to exercise choices and enjoy recreation and leisure across a range of times and places, he or she needs two different types of leisure behaviors.

1. Isolate (solitary)/individual skill activities that allow an individual to recreate in the absence of a formal time, place, or social context for recreation. For example, after completing participation in dinner clean-up activities in a group home, a person might still have two hours of discretionary leisure time until it is time to prepare for bed; or when arriving early for an appointment to have a haircut, an individual has ten minutes of discretionary time to use according to her personal preference. In traditional taxonomies, these activities are often categorized as hobbies, crafts, arts (Institute for Career and Leisure Development, 1978); object manipulation skills (Wehman, 1979); or sensory stimulation activities (Granger & Wehman, 1979). Regardless of how they are categorized, these activities are self-reinforcing: They are engaged in for the pleasure that is derived from the doing of them, and do not necessarily require a social context to be enjoyed.
2. Community (shared) participation activities is recreation which allows an individual to participate in a wide range of community-based recreation programs and events along with others. For example, an individual might wish to join a painting class, visit a museum, become a member of a ball club, or go on a camping trip. In traditional taxonomies, these activities might be called sports and physical development, play and games, outdoor activities, or entertainment and cultural events. Again, regardless of how these activities are formally clasified, they involve a social context, either through formal agencies outside the home, or through informal use of the social environments available at work, at home, or with community.

Youth who are deaf-blind and are in transition, then, have a need for at least two different types of leisure and recreation—isolate solitary leisure skills and community referenced recreation—and should have both types reflected in their daily lives.

Goals

The unique time, place, and personal choice characteristics of recreation/leisure also result in two different sets of goals for service providers. Programs that provide recreation/leisure services must aim to both increase specific skill levels of participants and increase the range of opportunities and access to participation available to participants.

1. Increasing range of skills. A growing literature is documenting the role of choice in influencing both competence and pleasure in an activity (Datillo & Rusch, 1985; Guess, Benson, & Siegel-Causey, 1985; Shevin & Klein, 1984). In order to make meaningful choices, an individual must have a range of behaviors to select among.

If an individual has a limited number of skills, and he often spends his free time in repetitive self-stimulating behavior, it is a disservice to say that this is a preferred activity that the individual has chosen, and therefore his leisure needs have been met. Choice requires alternatives; alternatives require skill acquisition and mastery before an individual can be honestly said to have exercised his personal preference among a range of alternatives. Service providers must therefore be prepared to teach new skills (be they solitary or group participation activities) so that a person will have genuine recreation and leisure options.

2. Increasing range of opportunity/access. In addition to possessing the skills required to engage in a recreation/leisure activity, a second essential element of choosing meaningful recreation is the availability of, or access to, the context in which the recreation and leisure can take place. Developing an individual's reading skills is pointless without access to books; learning ball handling skills is purposeless if the individual cannot use his local recreation center, school playground, or neighborhood gyms. Recreation service providers must therefore not only provide new skills to the individual transition-aged student with dual sensory impairments, but they must also broaden the leisure opportunities available to him.

The service needs of transition-aged youth with severe multiple handicaps and their families are thus at least fourfold: these persons must have leisure and recreation repertoires that include both individualized isolated leisure and social context recreation activities; furthermore, service providers must offer both increased skill acquisition or learning, and increased opportunities to utilize these skills in the appropriate contexts.

Model Indicators/Best Practices: What Are They?

Having outlined what I believe are some essential and unique components of recreation/leisure, and what at least four major consumer service needs are, I would now like to address what we do know as "best practice" or "state of the art" practices in meeting these needs in educational (public school) settings. A number of authors have documented different aspects of these model practices with transition-aged youth and adults with severe multiple handicaps, including Hamre-Nietupski and her colleagues in Iowa (Hamre-Nietupski, Nietupski, Sandvig, Sandvig, & Ayres, 1984; Nietupski, Hamre-Nietupski & Ayres, 1984; Nietupski & Svoboda, 1982); and Schleien and his colleagues in Minnesota (Schleien & Larson, in press; Schleien, Olson, Rogers, & McLafferty, 1985; Schleien, Rynders, Mustonen, Fox, A., & Kelterborn, B., 1986; Schleien, Wehman, & Kiernan, 1981). Some of these practices are drawn from public school programs in the San Francisco Bay Area and include at least one federally funded model demonstration project, which I direct, that works specifically with students who are deaf-blind (Project CIPSSI, Community Intensive Programming for Students with Sensory Impairments, USOE Grant #G008430094). CIPSSI's goal is to develop and evaluate a model for inclusion of students with multiple profound disabilities, including dual sensory impairment, in a community-intensive (community-based), functional life skills educational program.

Voeltz et al. (1982) identified three global areas of concern in developing recreation and leisure curricula for persons with severe disabilities: normalization, individualization, and logistical environmental factors. I would like to expand upon each of these in terms of specific model indicators or "best practices."

Normalization includes at least the following concerns:

Integration with nondisabled peers. The benefits of integrated school programs, for both severely disabled and nondisabled students, have by now been widely documented. These include attitude change, positive affect, and increased motivation (Hamilton & Anderson, 1983; Park & Goetz, 1985; Voeltz, 1982; see also Taylor, 1982 for general review). Examples of integrated recreation programming range from a deaf-blind adolescent mainstreamed into a P.E. class to a five-year-old participating in a kindergarten art activity at his school.

The dimension of integration, of course, raises questions about the role of "special" recreation programs, such as Special Olympics. The advantages of Special Olympics (increasing public awareness, providing success experiences, etc.) have been reviewed (Putnam et al., 1985) and should not be ignored. However, Special Olympics participation clearly cannot function as a lifelong leisure program for participants, any more than the Olympics serve as a lifelong recreation event for nondisabled participants. Special Olympics, therefore, cannot be the whole of an individual's recreation experience. If the dimension of choice is to be genuinely present, "special" recreation and leisure programs must be only one alternative among many others that include participation with nondisabled peers in "generic" recreation/leisure environments.

Chronological age-appropriate activities. Is the activity provided being taught something a nonhandicapped person would enjoy doing in his free time? (Brown et al., 1979). Nondisabled teenagers go to aerobics classes; nondisabled preschoolers play "Gotcha" and "Chicken Out," so these are activities we use in our school programs. This indicator is in direct contrast to a philosophy that says leisure can be anything an individual chooses. It is my experience that individuals with sensory impairments and severe handicaps "choose" age-inappropriate activities (i.e., light-gazing or finger-flicking) in part when they lack the skills to entertain themselves in other ways. In deciding on activities and contexts to teach as alternatives, age-appropriateness is a major normalization factor.

Referenced to NH peers. Providing and/or teaching skills, games, and leisure activities that are attractive, as well as appropriate, to chronological age peers is a further factor that facilitates normalization (Gaylor-Ross, Haring, Breen, & Pitts-Conway, 1984). When we go into the kindergarten with "Roger the Robot" adapted to a special switch, our students are provided with an entry into ongoing play; when a student shows up during lunch hour at the high school wearing a walkman, he gains access to the social context much more readily.

Occurrence in natural environments (Brown, et al, 1979). How much fun can playing baseball be if you can only use a plastic bat, and only hit the ball so hard because you "need" to learn baseball in the structured and safe environment of the classroom before you are "ready" to play baseball in the park? Using and/or teaching a recreation/leisure skills where it is needed makes sense in terms of learning efficiency and generalization problems (Sailor & Guess, 1983), but also in terms of motivation and fun, which is after all what recreation is supposed to provide. Turning the pages of a talking book is a bigger turn-on in the library with other kids your own age than it is at a desk in the classroom with your teacher.

Increase community access/participation. Recreation and leisure programs and/or activities that are integrated, chronologically age-appropriate, attractive to nondisabled peers, and occur in natural environments and social contexts will probably accomplish this last normalization criterion without any additional planning. Using a vending machine during a break at work, joining a game of Duck-Duck-Goose with the third graders, hanging out after lunch at local high school, going for a workout at the local gym, using a switch to listen to a radio while traveling to the park, and having a burger at McDonald's with your friends are all forms of leisure and recreation that enhance quality of life through normalized activity options.

Individualization includes at least the following concerns:

Respecting/facilitating choice. The unique role of choice in recreation/leisure behaviors has already been pointed out. Persons with severe multiple handicaps currently have relatively few options for choice and self-determination; as the field is attempting

123

to expand the role of preference in educational programs, leisure is a prime starting point. Preliminary evidence suggests that severely handicapped persons may experience greater pleasure when they select (in contrast to being assigned) to engage in a leisure activitiy (Datillo & Rusch, 1985); simply assigning an activity to someone to "enjoy" based solely upon its sensory feedback characteristics or motoric response requirements disregards the role of personal preference that is a hallmark of recreation activities.

If an individual has a range of recreation options (i.e., a variety of activities in which she is competent, or thats she can engage in with support or assistance), and she, upon occasion, chooses to engage in an activity that is not highly normalized, the recreation/leisure domain allows us to respect that choice. Integration of a person with disabilities into natural recreation environments requires adaptations on both sides. Too often, however, "choice," "preference," and "pleasure" are offered as a rationale for failing to teach new skills, which, in turn, further restricts genuine leisure options.

Increasing competence/skill acquisition. The role of competence in determining pleasure from an activity has long been addressed in the child development and infant literature (Harter, 1978; Ramey & Watson, 1972), and has recently received increasing attention in educational practices with learners with severe handicaps (Goetz, Schuler, & Sailor, 1982). People enjoy doing the things they are good at, and therefore one focus of an individualized leisure or recreational program should be to teach new skills and improve competence, so that activities can actually be enjoyable leisure options. Individuals with significant sensory and other handicaps may need to learn to play through structured, systematic instruction before the skill or activity can become a genuine recreation/leisure choice. (While recreation and leisure activities can often provide an excellent context for learning other skills such as motor skills, this is an educational issue that is secondary to the need for recreation and leisure activities, the primary purpose of which is to provide recreation and leisure.)

Addressing both individual/isolate and group context leisure needs. Every individual is entitled to a variety of recreation and leisure skills, such as activating a toy, listening to a record, working leathercraft, roller skating around the street, collecting stamps, or just painting fingernails, and group context recreation such as joining a "wave the parachute" game during recess, taking a swim class at the local Y, playing cards with siblings, or participating in a pep rally at the local college campus. Varied options are in direct contrast to what might be termed the "single solution" approach to leisure, in which all participants must participate in the same predetermined activity regardless of skill levels or interest levels, or in which leisure means doing the same thing at the same time in the same place because it is "leisure" time or "break" time.

Based upon individual and family style. An individual whose family enjoys playing table games will have little opportunity for increased participation if he primarily learns calisthenics and weightlifting skills in his recreation program. Conversely, an individual whose family spends a great deal of time outdoors hiking and camping will be poorly served by a leisure program that focuses upon clay modeling. Family preference is a significant planning factor, as are individual preference and individual skill levels. Assessment practices that address these issues are beyond the scope of this paper, and the reader is referred to Certo, Schleien and Humber (1983), and Wuerch and Voeltz (1982) for further discussion.

Logistical environmental factors. This area of concern addresses the practical matters of availability, expense, and safety of any given program or activity. A leisure program that is inaccessible to an individual through readily available transporation may be a luxury, and not truly functional long-term recreation. Leisure activities that involve costly equipment and/or materials may greatly enhance an individual's quality of life (e. g., a lift harness to provide access to a therapeutic swimming pool) but the burden of these costs has to be shared and costly alternatives cannot be the sole alternatives available. Safety factors must be weighed against the dignity of risk: going to the soda fountain to enjoy a coke poses risks to a young girl who has been described as "medically fragile," but these risks must be weighed against the pleasure and self-esteem of being "just another third grader."

These examples of model indicators do not just "happen." Successful recreation and leisure, in which experiences are individualized, contribute to skill acquisition, reflect community norms, and facilitate interaction and participation with nondisabled peers, require several key elements. For example, the environments in which these people are recreating have been prepared through conscious inservice/staff development/awareness activities, and the personnel working with these students have training in individualized assessment and data based instructional procedures. I will return to these points later in the paper.

Current Status of Adult Services

Data on the status of leisure and recreation activities and programs for adults with profound handicaps including dual sensory impairment is extremely limnited. Some investigations have looked at leisure participation of persons with moderate to severe handicaps subsequent to deinstitutionalization or after leaving high school (Birenbaum & Re, 1979; Chesseldine & Jeffree, 1981; Gollay, Freedman, Wyngaarden, & Kurtz, 1978; Hill & Bruininks, 1981; Intaglia, Willer & Wicks, 1981), but even this data base is not comprehensive.

The literature that is available concerning individuals with moderate to severe disabilities does suggest at least three major factors influencing recreation/leisure lifestyles for young adults:

1. Families often shoulder the major responsibility for providing recreation and leisure activities and opportunities since personal friendships decline after individuals leave their school programs (Chesseldine & Jeffree, 1981).
2. Neither a successful vocational placement nor a successful community residential placement in itself guarantees a normalized leisure lifestyle (Birenbaum & Re, 1979; Intaglia et al., 1981).
3. Lack of participation in leisure activities is often due to practical factors, such as not having adequate transportation or not having someone to accompany the individual if needed (Hill & Bruininks, 1981) but is also often due to lack of skills in utilizing available leisure opportunities (Birenbaum & Re, 1979; Hill & Bruininks, 1981).

Clearly these three factors suggest that planned, systematic service delivery is going to be needed in order to accomplish effective recreation and leisure for deaf-blind youth in transition. Because leisure may occur at varied times and places when the individual is at home or at work, and because leisure is a matter of pleasure and personal choice, it appears that other agencies responsible for residential and vocational placement do not regard leisure as their primary responsibility. As a result, the data suggest that an individual's recreation/leisure needs often go unmet or are met solely by the individual's family.

What about the perspective of service providers and agencies whose primary responsibility is recreation and leisure for all citizens, including those with disabilities? The need for a comprehensive community service delivery system of recreation and leisure programming for persons with disabilities has been expressed in the literature (McGregor, 1982). However, in many instances, generic service agencies such as park and recreation agencies appear to be unaware of their roles and responsibilities in providing services (Austin, Peterson, Peccarelli, Binkley, & Lacker, 1977; Edgington, Compton, Ritchie, & Vederman, 1975; Schleien, Porter, & Wehman, 1979). As an example, Schleien and Werder (1985) recently completed a comprehensive survey of service providers in Minnesota.

Schleien and Werder included 323 public schools, park and recreation agencies, and community education agencies (all tax supported) in their needs assessment survey. Among their major findings were the following:

1. Each agency type believed that another agency should have primary responsibility for meeting the needs of citizens with disabilities.
2. Services offered were limited in both quantity and quality: recreational activities available to citizens with disabilities were based on instructor preferences rather than client preferences, and were not referenced to individual needs or skill levels; services also tended to be restricted to activities that were stereotyped "handicapped" activities (field trips) versus more normalizing activities (camping or spectator sports); and services were generally not integrated with nondisabled participants.
3. Less than 10% of the agencies employed a full-time professional to develop and implement programs for individuals with special needs.

Based on these findings, Schleien and Werder made a number of recommendations, including either transagency models or designation of a lead agency, such as, parks and recreation programs. Schleien and Werder also recommended increased support for training personnel, and that offered recreation services be consistent with a number of "best practives" that are outlined earlier in this paper.

When I was asked to prepare this paper, I also completed a small local phone survey of my own. While generalizations are not appropriate, I was surprised to find many similar concerns to those expressed by Schleien's respondents. My sample included both park and recreation agencies (five recreation centers in San Francisco), the public library branch, and two private nonprofit agencies (YMCA and the Jewish Community Center). In every instance, when asked about including, enrolling, or serving an individual with extensive special needs within their regularly provided programs, the agency indicated no anticipated difficulties and did not refer me to a "handicapped only" program. In each instance, the agency requested that supervision be provided so that the participant could benefit from the activity being offered. Thus, a willingness to serve, but coupled with lack of information, leadership, or perceived responsibility for facilitating participation, concurs with some of Schleien's findings as well.

What's Next?

In summarizing the various findings from adult and generic service providers, while keeping in mind the "best practices" characteristics that should be present when providing services, I suggest that at least the following needs must be addressed if transition-aged youth with handicaps of deafness and blindness and their families are to enjoy a genuine leisure lifestyle:

1. Expand the role of recreation as a related service, and mandate inclusion of recreation and leisure program services in IEPs (Individual Educational Plan under PL 94-142) and ITPs (Individual Transition Plans) for transition-aged youth. The National Consortium in Physical Education and Recreation for the Handicapped (Ramey & Watson, 1985) has discussed many of these issues in a position paper prepared for the Office of Special Education Programs.
2. Designate a lead agency with primary responsibility for providing appropriate recreation/leisure activities, opportunities, and skill acquisition to persons with severe multiple handicaps. By designating a generic agency (i. e., one that serves all citizens) many of the model practices can be more easily accomplished than they could be by utilizing a "special" service agency. Schleien and Werder suggest that Parks and Recreation be the lead agency. I think this is one of many issues we can discuss at this conference.

3. Within the designate lead agency, explore and develop new professional roles that will enable the agency to successfully serve persons with profound disabilities. Some alternatives to consider might include the following:

"Recreation coaches" based upon the model of job coaches (Wehman, Hill, Goodall, Cleveland, Brooke, & Pentecost, 1982), whose role is to identify and match client to job, provide initial intensive job training, and then be available for intermittent follow up in the workplace. Similarly, a recreation coach's role might be to match individualized participant needs with a set of existing programs, provide skill training as needed to the participant and to the service provider, and to provide follow up on an intermittent basis and continue to create new opportunities in accord with individual and family preference or needs.

"Supported Recreation" based upon the model of supported work for those individuals with significant disabilities that preclude complete independence in the workplace (Brown et al., 1983). A supported recreation model is appropriate for those persons who require ongoing assistance to enjoy and benefit from structured recreation/leisure programs. As in the supported work model, a number of different persons might actually provide this support (a co-participant) with the professional providing initial intensive training. The notion of "companionships" (Salzberg & Langford, 1981) in which disabled and nondisabled persons are matched on the basis of shared leisure interests is another option which enables persons with significant disabilities to be full participants in recreation and leisure.

4. Prepare community agencies through inservice and awareness training prior to actually providing services. An extensive literature exists on how to integrate persons with handicaps into a "generic" agency such as a public school. Models for awareness training of co-participants, extensive media, and resource libraries are available and have been demonstrated to influence the success of an integration effort (Sailor, Anderson, & Halvorsen, 1985). Similar materials need to be developed that are appropriate to community service agencies and indeed some are already underway (Bullock, 1986; Schleien & Ray, 1986). Once developed, this process should occur on a systematic basis with all generic service providers.

5. Provide personnel training in the areas of therapeutic recreation, adaptive P. E., and special education to close the gaps between professional areas of expertise and to prepare persons for new professional roles (#2 above). Currently, therapeutic recreation professionals have strengths in the areas of adapting activities and utilizing community resources; however, they may be unfamiliar with both the new population they will be asked to serve and with the philosophy of model practices in services for these individuals. Conversely, special education personnel may have extensive knowledge of specialized needs and training procedures but are often unaware of the resource available in the "generic" community.

Given the size of the task, this is a fairly short list of recommendations. Major issues, including costs, responsibility for program monitoring, and family involvement with adult service agencies have not been addressed. Principles of partial participation and adaptation (Baumgart et al., 1982) and structured individualized instruction (Sailor & Guess, 1983), both of which are integral to effective services for persons with multiple profound disabilities, have barely been touched upon. However, I hope that I've made a convincing case that an individual's recreation and leisure needs are every bit as crucial and valid as his or her need to live in an appropriate and comfortable residential setting and to work at a job that provides social and economic compensation. The fact that leisure occurs in, around, and between all the other things that we do in no way decreases its importance in determining quality of life for everyone.

References

Austin, D., Peterson, J., Peccarelli, L., Binkley, A., & Lacker, M. (1977). Therapeutic recreation in Indiana: Health through recreation. Bloomington, Indiana University, Department of Recreation and Park Administration.

Baumgart, D., Brown, L., Pumpian, I., Nisbet, J., Ford, A., Sweet, M., Messina, R., & Schroeder, J. (1982). Principle of partial participation and individualized adaptations in educational programs for severly handicapped students. Journal of the Association for Persons with Severe Handicaps, 7, 17-27.

Birenbaum, A. & Re, M. (1979). Resettling mentally retarded adults in the community-- almost four years later. American Journal of Mental Deficiency, 83, 323-329.

Brown, L., Branston, M., Baumgart, D., Vincent, L., Falvey, M., & Schroeder, G. (1979). Using the characteristics of current and subsequent least restrictive environments in the development of curricular content for severly handicapped students. AAESPH Review, 4, 407-424.

Brown, L., Branston, M., Hamre-Nietupski, S., Pumpian, I., Certo, N., & Gruenewald, L. (1979). A strategy for developing chronological age appropriate and functional curricular content for severely handicapped adolescents and young adults. Journal of Special Education, 13, 81-90.

Brown, L., Shiraga, B., Ford, A., Nisbet, J., Van Deventer, P., Sweet, M., York, J., & Loomis, R. (1983). In L. Brown, A. Ford, J. Nisbet et al. (Eds.), Educational programs for severely handicapped students: Vol, 13. Madison WI: Madison Metropolitan School District.

Bull, C. (1972). Prediction of future daily behaviors: An empirical measure of leisure. Journal of Leisure Research, 4, 119-128.

Bullock, C. (1986). Project Life (Leisure is for Everyone). Chapel Hill: University of North Carolina, Department of Recreation Administration.

Certo, N., Schleien, S., & Hunter, D. (1983). An ecological assessment inventory to facilitate community recreation participation by severely disabled individuals. Therapeutic Recreation Journal, 17, 29-38.

Chesseldine, S., & Jeffree, D. (1981). Mentally handicapped adolescents: Their use of leisure. Journal of Mental Deficiency Research, 25, 49-59.

Compton, D., Burrows, M., & Witt, P. (1979). Facilitating play and recreation opportu- nities for deaf blind children and youth. Dallas: North Texas State University, South Central Regional Center.

Datillo, J., & Barnett, L. (1985). Therapeutic recreation for individuals with severe handicaps. Journal of the Association for Persons with Severe Handicaps, 10, 194-199.

Donellan, A., Mirenda, P., Mesaros, R., & Fassbender, L. (1984). Analyzing the communi- cative functions of aberrant behaviors. Journal of the Association for Persons with Severe Handicaps, 9, 201-212.

Edgington, C., Compton, D., Ritchie, A., & Vederman, R. (1975). The status of services for special populations in park and recreation departments in the state of Iowa. Therapeutic Recreation Journal, 3, 109-116.

Gaylord-Ross, R., Haring, T., Breen, C., & Pitts-Conway, V. (1984). The training and generalization of social interaction skills with autistic youth. Journal of Applied Behavior Analysis, 17, 229-248.

Goetz, L., Schuler, A., & Sailor, W. (1982). Functional competence as a factor in communication instruction. Exceptional Education Quarterly, 2, 51-61.

Gollay, E., Freedman, R., Wyngaarden, J., & Kurtz, N. (1978). Coming back: The community experiences of deinstitutionalized mentally retarded people. Cambridge, MA: Ab+ Books.

Granger, C., & Wehman, P. (1979). Sensory stimulation. In P. R. Wehman (Ed.), Recreation programming for developmentally disabled persons. Baltimore: University Park Press.

Guess, D., Benson, H., & Siegel-Causey, E. (1985). Concepts and issues related to choice-making and autonomy among persons with severe handicaps. Journal of the Association for Persons with Severe Handicaps, 10, 79-86.

Hamilton, E., & Anderson, S. (1983). Effects of leisure activities on attitudes toward people with disabilities. Theraeutic Recreation Journal, 17, 50-57.

Hamre-Nietupski, S., Nietupski, J., Sandvig, R., Sandvig, M., & Ayres, B. (1984). Leisure skills instruction with deaf/blind severely handicapped young adults in a community residential setting. The Journal of the Association for Persons with Severe Handicaps, 9, 49-54.

Harter, S. (1978). Effectance motivation reconsidered. Human Development, 21, 34-64.

Hill, B., & Bruininks, R. (1981). Family, leisure, and social activities of mentally retarded people in residential facilities. Minneapolis: University of Minnesota, Developmental Disabilities Project on Residential Services and Community Adjustment.

Intaglia, J., Willer, B., & Wicks, N. (1981). Factors related to the quality of community adjustment in family care homes. In R. Bruininks, C. Meyers, B. Sigford, & K. Lakin (Eds.), Deinstitutionalization and community adjustment of mentally retarded people. Washington, D. C.: American Association on Mental Deficiency.

McGregor, G. (1982). Leisure and the domaines of home, school and the community. In P. Verhoven, S. Schleien, & M. Bender (Eds.), Leisure education and the handicapped individual: An ecological perspective. Washington, D. C.: Institute for Career and Leisure Development.

Murphy, J. F. (1981). Concepts of leisure. Englewood Cliffs, N. J.: Prentice Hall.

Nietupski, J., Hamre-Nietupski, S., & Ayres, B. (1984). Review of task analytic leisure skill training efforts: Practioner implications and future research needs. Journal of the Association for Persons with Severe Handicaps, 9, 88-97.

Park, H. S., & Goetz, L. (1985). Affect of young adults with severe disabilities in two differing educational programs. Manuscript submitted for publication.

Putnam, J., Werder, J., & Schleien, S. (1985). Leisure and recreation services for handicapped persons. In K. Lakin & R. Bruininks (Eds.), Strategies for achieving community integration of developmentally disabled citizens. Baltimore: Paul Brookes.

Ramey, S., & Watson, J. (1972). Nonsocial reinforcement of infant's vocalization. Child Development, 42, 291-297.

Ramey, S., & Watson, J. (1985). Recreation as a related service for students with handicapping conditions. Washington, D. C.: Office of Special Education Programs, National Consortium on Physical Education and Recreation for the Handicapped.

Sailor, W., Anderson, J., & Halvorsen, A. (1985). The California Research Institute on Integration of Students with Severe Disabilities: Annual Report. San Francisco: San Francisco State University.

Sailor, W., & Guess, D. (1983). Severely handicapped students: An instructional design. Boston: Houghton-Mifflin.

Salzberg, C., & Langford, C. (1981). Community integration of mentally retarded adults through leisure activity. Mental Retardation, 19, 127-131.

Schleien, S., & Larson, A. (1986). Adult leisure education for the independent use of a community recreation center. Journal of the Association for Persons with Severe Handicaps, 11, 39-44.

Schleien, S., & Ray, M. T. (1986). Integrating persons with disabilities into community leisure services. Minneapolis: University of Minnesota, Division of Recreation, Park, and Leisure Studies.

Schleien, S., Olson, K., Roger, N., & McLafferty, M. (1985). Integrating children with severe handicaps into recreation and physical education programs. Journal of Park and Recreation Administration, 3(1), 50-66.

Schleien, S., Porter, J., & Wehman, P. (1979). An assessment of the leisure skill needs of developmentally disabled individuals. Therapeutic Recreation Journal, 13, 16-21.

Schleien, S., Rynders, J., Mustonen, T., Fox, A., & Kelterborn, B. (1986). Use of a multi-element design to determine the effects of social levels of play on learners with autism. Manuscript submitted for publication.

Schleien, S., Wehman, P., & Kiernan, J. (1981). Teaching leisure skills to severely handicapped adults: An age-appropriate darts game. Journal of Applied Behavior Analysis, 14, 513-519.

Schleien, S., & Werder, J. (1985). Perceived responsibilities of special recreation services in Minnesota. Therapeutic Recreation Journal, 19, 51-62.

Shevin, M., & Klein, N. (1984). The importance of choice-making skills for students with severe disabilities. Journal of the Association for Persons with Severe Handicaps, 9, 159-166.

Taylor, S. (1982). From segregation to integration: Strategies for integrating severely handicapped students in normal school and community settings. Journal of the Association for Persons with Severe Handicaps, 7, 42-49.

Voeltz, L. (1982). Effects of structured interactions with severely handicapped peers on children's attitudes. American Journal of Mental Deficiency, 86, 380-390.

Voeltz, L., Wuerch, B., & Wilcox, B. (1982). Leisure and recreation: Preparation for independence, integration, and self-fulfillment. In B. Wilcox & T. Bellamy (Eds.), Design of high school programs for severely handicapped students. Baltimore: Paul Brookes.

Wehman, P. (1979). Recreation programming for developmentally disabled persons. Baltimore: University Park Press.

Wehman, P., Hill, M., Goodall, P., Cleveland, P., Brooke, V., & Pentecost, J. (1982). Job placement and follow up of moderately and severely handicapped individuals after three years. Journal of the Association for Persons with Severe Handicaps, 7, 5-16.

Wehman, P., & Schleien, S. (1981). Leisure programs for handicapped persons: Adaptations, techniques and curriculum. Baltimore: University Park Press.

Wuerch, B., & Voeltz, L. (1982). Longitudinal leisure skills for severely handicapped learners: The ho'onanea curriculum. Baltimore: Paul Brookes.

In Response to Lori Goetz

Importance of Communication Skills and Their Etiology in
Planning of Recreation and Leisure Programs for Persons with
Multiple/Profound Handicaps of Deafness and Blindness

Pamela Mathy-Laikko and Terrence R. Dolan

Introduction

I believe my role on this panel is to contribute the perspectives of an administrator of a university-based facility whose programs are concerned with the topic of deaf-blindness. I am the director of the Waisman Center on Mental Retardation and Human Development at the University of Wisconsin. The Waisman Center is comprised of a Mental Retardation Research Center (MRRC) and a University Affiliated Facility (UAF). As you probably know, there are eleven federally funded MRRCs in the United States--each conducting basic and clinical research on development of the nervous system and on abnormal developmental processes. Also, there are about 48 UAFs in the United States funded either by the training division of Maternal and Child Health or the Administration on Developmental Disabilities. These UAFs conduct interdisciplinary training and clinical/educational service programs on behalf of persons with developmental disabilities.

I might add, secondarily, that I am a psychologist interested in perception, particularly auditory perception, so my interests and earlier scientific endeavors are related to the topic we are discussing.

I was impressed with the comments made by Dr. Lori Goetz this afternoon. In a succinct presentation, she has identified some key issues for our consideration; she has placed her comments within the context of the currently available literature on the subject, and she has made some pointed and interesting recommendations for future actions. What I would like to do in the next eight or nine minutes to to contribute comments or suggestions related to three areas mentioned in her presentation.

First, I suggest that our discussion of recreation and leisure programs for those who are deaf-blind should include a more concerted discussion of the individual differences that these individuals bring to a recreation and leisure program, especially the unique communication barriers associated with deaf-blindness.

Second, I have some specific comments concerning the issue of definitions, the integration of deaf-blind and noncompromised children and adults; and the issue of choice-making.

Third, I wish to emphasize one of Dr. Goetz's concluding points concerning the need for training (or, more accurately, for training and advocacy) associated with programs for persons with deaf-blind handicaps.

Comment #1

Dr. Goetz has addressed what she refers to as the best components or "best practices" in recreation and leisure programs, and has referred to many important components in those programs. I suggest that consideration of communication skills, the etiology of those communication skills, and the individual differences associated with those elements are equally critical variables.

In a presentation which dealt with special needs of persons with deaf-blindness and which was intended for use by rehabilitation counselors, teachers and other professionals working with persons with deaf-blindness, Koner and Rice (1984) divided deaf-blindness into four categories to be used "as a system in the search for a more individualized understanding of the deaf-blind person." The categories are based upon the time of onset of the combined disability, and include the following:

1. Congenitally deaf, adventitiously blind: the person who has been deaf since birth or early childhood and loses sight in adult life (e.g., a person with Usher's Syndrome);
2. Congenitally deaf-blind: the person who has been both deaf and blind from birth or early childhood (e.g., shows effects of maternal rubella);
3. Adventitiously deaf-blind: the person who loses both sight and hearing in adult life (e.g., through trauma, injury, etc.);
4. Congenitally blind, adventitiously deaf: the person who has been blind from birth or early childhood and loses hearing in adult life (e.g., a person with retrolental fibroplasia).

These categories are presented here as a brief illustration of the diversity of challenges that individuals who are deaf-blind may present to a recreation/leisure program. For example, a congenitally deaf-blind person with concomitant profound mental retardation, who has never participated in a recreation program, may need to be taught recreation skills. However, a person who has lost the use of one or the other or both senses adventitiously may need to learn new ways to participate in activities that he/she previously enjoyed and/or learn new activities.

In addition to considering the onset of the disability, recreational assessments and training programs might also consider in their planning the impact of other disabilities that are frequently associated with deaf-blindness (especially deaf-blindness of congenital onset). These include mental retardation and physical impairments. Also, it has been well documented that persons with deaf-blindness present unique receptive and expressive communication barriers and that these barriers also affect persons who attempt to communicate with them (for example, see discussions in Jensema, 1979 a, 1979 b, 1980, 1981; Curtis & Donlon, 1984; Konar & Rice, 1984).

This paper was presented by Terrence R. Dolan.

In summary, it is suggested that we consider carefully the etiological, cognitive, social and communicative characteristics of individuals as we plan future programs.

Comment #2

I would like to respond to three specific points made by Dr. Goetz. At the beginning of her presentation, Dr. Goetz discussed the definitions of leisure and of recreation, particularly from the perspective that the usual definitions do not provide much in the way of substantive and concrete information to be used by agencies and/or individuals seeking to improve recreation and leisure services for a specified group of people. Dr. Goetz attempts to pin down a definition of recreation/leisure by describing several components: (1) recreation and leisure takes place during discretionary time (nonwork time); (2) it can occur in variable locations; (3) it is defined as being a personally preferred activity; and (4) recreation/leisure activities can either be solitary activities or activities that one does in a social context (in the company of others). In defining recreation/leisure by time, place, and personal preference, the actual activities that may constitute recreation/leisure are left open. The "open-endedness" seems to serve a useful function in that it allows for a great deal of individual variablity in choice. However, such an open-ended definition may not suffice when considering its use by an educational or community agency responsible for recreation/leisure programs for persons with deaf-blindness. As discussed earlier, persons with deaf-blindness comprise a heterogeneous group for whom recreational activities encompass a broad range. One might consider, as a starting point, doing a study to collect information about what activities this population currently includes in its recreation/leisure repertoire. This information could be used to supplement existing data on recreational activities for various age groups. Such a list of activities could be used as a guideline which staff could use to develop, modify, and add new items to programs when necessary.

My concern here is that a definition that is too open-ended is subject to misuse. Although it may be useful in encouraging creativity, it may also encourage apathy on the part of agencies and organizations (particularly in a time of reduced resources). An agency, for example, could argue that it already has appropriate recreation/leisure programs because it satisfies the definition when, in fact, its program consists of large unstructured periods of time when the individuals just sit and do nothing.

In the middle of her presentation, Dr. Goetz discussed the importance of the integration of the person with deaf-blindness with nondisabled peers. Such integration, unless carefully planned, may not produce the anticipated benefits to deaf-blind individuals nor to their nondisabled partners. As mentioned earlier, persons with deaf-blindness have unique communication barriers. These barriers must be overcome in some manner, including perhaps the training of sign language and/or the used of alternative communication systems. In turn, the nondisabled peer must learn to receive and transmit information in an equally appropriate mode.

I know of no studies that have examined the social interactions among adults or children with deaf-blindness and their nondisabled peers. However, research has been done examining social interactions among five preschool children (ages 4-5) with severe-to-profound hearing impairments and five, same-age, nondisabled children (Arnold & Tremblay, 1979). All the children were enrolled in an integrated preschool program. A sample of playground behavior of each child was recorded on videotape and analyzed. Tapes were coded for the frequency of occurrence and initiator/receivor roles for nine behaviors (vocalizations, gestures, approaches, physical contact, imitation/social play, give object, take object and aggression). The results indicated that hearing children were more likely to approach, engage in social play, vocalize to, and physically contact other hearing children. In contrast, the children with hearing impairments showned no definite peer preference. The authors concluded that nondisabled children may have found attempts to interact with hearing-impaired peers less socially reinforcing because of their lack of comparable communication skills.

The results of the above study suggest that successful integration programs must consider the communication skills of the participants. It may be that more successful groupings would be comprised of individuals of different chronological ages but who are matched in communicative ability. Preliminary results of research now being conducted at the Waisman Center suggest that this is so.

Dr. Goetz also suggested the importance of the component of choice in the conduct of recreation/leisure activities. That is, it is important for the participant to be involved in choosing the activity. I concur. The process of selection, however, may be complex and the results may be misinterpreted. Children with a conventional language system (e.g., sign language) may understand all of the options available to them and communicate their choice effectively. Persons without such communicative skills may not understand the range of opportunities available and/or have difficulty communicating their final choice. It may be that the development of new techniques to assess the wishes and attractions of these persons without a conventional communication technique, based upon observation of that person in various situations, may assist in deducing the choice the individual makes. Research is needed to develop such effective assessment techniques.

Comment #3

Concerning my last comment, Dr. Goetz made a point about the need for training programs to improve and increase the recreation/leisure opportunities for persons with deaf-blindness. I strongly endorse her recommendations and suggest that such programs are needed for both professionals and paraprofessionals. I believe that these training programs should stress the development and use of communication techniques used by persons with deaf-blindness, observational assessment techniques, and the range of variability of behavioral characteristics associated with deaf-blind persons with differing etiologies, cognitive status, communication ability, and communication mode.

Finally, how do these considerations affect the role, or potential role of university-based programs (MRRCs, UAFs, R & T Center, etc.)? I believe these programs have a responsibility to become more involved in the development of such training programs as well as in their advocacy. The Waisman Center is not unlike many other UAFs. At the Waisman Center, there are scientists and clinicians from psychology, engineering, physiology, speech/language, audiology, counseling, rehabilitative medicine, and many other disciplines, who are involved in research and programming for persons with developmental disabilities and a concommitant communications impairment. These experts have the capability and experiences to conduct interdisciplinary research on problems associated with deaf-blindness, and some are experienced in the conduct of clinical and educational programs designed to work with persons with deaf-blindness. They also conduct training programs for professionals and paraprofessionals within their respective regions, and they conduct technical assistance and consultation programs in which they collaborate with the various agencies and organizations that work with persons with developmental disabilities. I believe it is important for UAFs and other univeristy programs to make a more concerted effort in training and consultative efforts pertaining to recreation and leisure programs for persons who are deaf-blind, and to work with those agencies who are responsible for such programs.

How we may contribute, and the specifics of what needs to be done by all agencies and organizations, I assume, will come out of discussions such as those you are having there now. I believe that discussions at conferences such as this one, and papers such as the one contributed by Dr. Goetz a few moments ago, can provide the basis for effective planning and, subsequently, to more effective recreation/leisure programs.

References

Arnold, D. & Trumblay, A. (1979). Interactions of deaf and hearing preschool children. Journal of Communication Disorders, 12, 245-251.

Curtis, W. S., & Donlon, E. T. (1984). A ten-year follow-up study of deaf-blind children. Exceptional Children, 50, 449-455.

Jensema, C. K. (1979). A review of communication systems used by deaf-blind people, part I. American Annals of the Deaf, 124, 720-725.

Jensema, C. K. (1979). A review of communication systems used by deaf-blind people, part II. American Annals of the Deaf, 124, 808-809.

Jensema, C. K. (1980). A review of communication systems used by deaf-blind people, part III. American Annals of the Deaf, 125, 9-10.

Jensema, C. K. (1981). Reports of communication method usage by teachers of deaf-blind children, American Annals of the Deaf, 126, 8-10.

Konar, U., & Rice, B. D. (Ed.). (1984). Strategies for Serving Deaf-Blind Clients (Eleventh Institute on Rehabilitation Issues). San Antonio, Texas: Arkansas Research & Training Center in Vocational Rehabilitation, University of Arkansas, Arkansas Rehabilitation Services.

In Response to Lori Goetz

A Parent's Viewpoint

Barbara Ryan

About four years ago I went through what's called a Parent Interview or "Significant Other" Interview. The reason for the interview is to establish the critical needs for the child and how to teach them. It takes into consideration what the parents feel is critical for that child.

As I went through that interview it went very nicely. They started out by asking me what my child was doing on a day-to-day basis, what my child did in the morning before she went to school, what she did when she got home. That hour went very nicely.

They asked what did she really like the most. I liked telling about that.

Then they went into, What does your child do that's special? What does your child do during the week that's special? What does your child do on the week-end that's special? I kind of went into a state of shock when that was asked, and some real guilt feelings hit me hard. Because I was at a new stage, I was in transition with my daughter going from childhood into adulthood.

It was easy for me when she was a child to have her doing recreational-leisure kinds of activities with the family because I had two other daughters. So it was a natural flow. It was a natural involvement and it felt really comfortable. Then my other two daughters grew older—they didn't need the family structure that was provided before, so there was a drop-off. And I was aware of it and didn't know quite how to handle it.

So it hit me when that was asked of me, face to face. They didn't mean to challenge me like that. They didn't realize that I went into emotional trauma on the inside, feeling very, very guilty because I really hadn't been providing my daughter with an ongoing recreational-leisure type program that was very planned.

There was no more swimming activity on a weekly basis. There was no more horseback riding because we had gotten rid of the horses. There was no more--we had gone hiking a lot. All those kinds of things that worked very well within our family unit were gone because the family changed. And I really had been feeling guilty about that. I felt guilty about it for a long time.

Today, I feel differently. I don't feel guilty any longer, even though I still don't plan anything systematically. I now don't feel that it's totally my responsibility. I can see where there are agencies and other people that are going to help me do this. And I have reached out and tried to provide my daughter with another person, other than myself, to entertain her and provide her with recreational-leisure time.

The thing I've done is this: I hired a companion for Doria. Besides having a live-in housekeeper to make sure that there is somebody in the household that provides her with her meals and makes sure she gets on the bus in the morning--that's kind of a very critical issue--I do have an age-appropriate companion for her. I found this person through the university that was close by. And it has worked out beautifully. And even though there are communication problems, somehow it works out beautifully when you have some commonalities. And the fact is, that my daughter is interested in boys, and she gets a big kick out of the fact when the companion brings her boyfriend over and she can giggle and flirt.

She does like going to movies. And this person is not as hung-up as I am about the noises she makes in movies. She thinks it's funny. I get kind of embarassed.

She gets excited and is happy to take my daughter down to the beach with her and do those kind of free-flowing recreational things. It has worked well. I was fortunate to find somebody that does a very, very good job, and that I can trust. And I know it's an ongoing challenge through the years. I'll have to keep finding companions for her . . . .

The challenge is even going to be greater as our children get older: how to provide age-appropriate recreational-leisure kinds of skills. The agencies that are responsible should be more responsible. They aren't aware of this responsibility yet, and I think it's going to be up to parents to make sure they do become aware of this responsibility.

There are some things they do provide, but we as care providers didn't know to ask for them. Transportation is a prime example of something that is available, at least through our developmental disabilities area, the regionals in California. Transportation is available for our people, but you have to ask for it. You have to practically demand it--it doesn't come easily.

Tying in parks and recreation, and going back to the communication factor, how are we going to improve those areas? I think probably having a primary person involved in these activities is essential, like having a companion. How do we train those companions? I don't know. That is something I think we're going to have to look at and we're going to have to deal with in a very, very specific way. I think it can be done. Actually I'm pretty excited about it.

As far as the ongoing education of our children goes, I've been very interested in the past few years about the Adaptive Physical Education coaches that have been involved in the educational system. I've been disappointed in them. I cannot begin to tell you how horrified I was to walk in and see what the Adaptive Physical Education teacher was doing with my daughter, and that was before I even knew about age-appropriate activities. The teacher had her crawling through little tunnels made for preschool children, and she was 14 or 15 years old. I mean that's not really very appropriate.

Start insisting that those agencies and those people that are trained in the Adaptive Physical Education teacher programs be more appropriate with our children as they are growing through the years.

There are other agencies that could be responsible for these recreation-leisure kind of activities. How about looking to the arts, all the different types of art, the dance, the music. And I know I'll be challenged by the fact that the children can't hear.

138

You're right, they can't hear. But my daughter is 21 now, and I do take her dancing, into a bar that has the flashing lights, that has the loud music, and she can stand right next to the speaker.

Now you have to keep an open mind about this because my daughter isn't going to dance. She does not like to dance. However, she is stimulated by the vibration and the flashing lights, and she does like to stand there on the dance floor. I'd like to find some nice looking young man to maybe dance around her and maybe hold her. She does like to slow dance, occasionally. And then she wouldn't look so bizarre, out in the public on a dance floor where there are social kinds of situations.

These kinds of issues, I think we need to really look at in depth. We need to look at the age-appropriate kinds of activities that are involved. We need to really work very, very hard at being daring and very, very willing to risk in our thinking about what is leisure and what is recreational.

Report of the Working Group on Recreation and Leisure

Group Members

Martin Adler	Norman McCallum
Terry Carr	Caye Nelson
John Datillo	Barbara Ryan
Terrance Dolan	Rosanne Silberman
Lillian Garcia	Nancy Trenbeth
Lori Goetz	Carol Wallenstein

Report prepared by Rosanne Silberman

Philosophy/Belief Statement

The goal of implementing recreation/leisure programs is to improve the quality of life for a person with deaf-blindness and other profound handicaps. We have defined some leisure needs, have suggested a number of characteristics of the desired recreation and leisure programs to meet these needs, and have addressed some avenues of implementation and logistical considerations. Each of these persons, from the lowest functioning level upward, must have access to frequent and consistent recreational/leisure programs. These programs are a priority in the realistic pursuit of developing an appropriate leisure lifestyle that overcomes unique communication barriers and, most importantly, enhances the individual's quality of life.

Recreation and leisure play a vital lifelong role in the lives of all human beings, including those who are deaf-blind, because recreation and leisure participation signficantly enhance the quality of life.

While the terms recreation and leisure are frequently used interchangeably, their meanings are actually quite different. Recreation refers to structured activities, either on an individual basis or in a group. One can get involved in recreational activities which may or may not include a leisure state. Leisure refers to a state of mind which gives the person choice and control and thereby allows him to experience enjoyment, pleasure, and satisfaction. The distinction between these two terms is an important consideration in planning recreation/leisure programs for these individuals.

Program Approach and Characteristics

Approach. Due to concomitant sensory and physiological deficits, isolation and poor self-image are inherent in the life of the person with deaf-blindness and other profound handicaps. These conditions must be counteracted by meeting the following needs within the areas of recreation and leisure. These include the need for the individual to

1. have exposure to opportunities for recreation and leisure on a daily basis;
2. Develop skills enabling participation at an optimal performance level;
3. develop isolate skills (e. g., press a switch to cause vibration or a cassette recorder to turn on);
4. develop interaction and group recreation skills;
5. be involved in chronological, age-appropriate recreation activities and materials;
6. be provided with opportunities to communicate choices and preferences;
7. be involved in interactions with others.

Characteristics. Recreational/Leisure Programs should

1. coordinate leisure with other aspects of a person's life (e. g., work and residential environments);
2. include individual and group participation options;
3. occur in variable locations, including natural environments such as the home or in a park;
4. provide opportunities for integration with nonhandicapped peers through reciprocal activities among participants;
5. provide appropriate transportation to and from a barrier-free location whenever necessary for the recreation activity;
6. be future oriented and be sensitive to preferences of the family and significant others;
7. focus on the development of lifelong skills;
8. provide for a range of skills to facilitate development of a repertoire of leisure opportunities;
9. encourage the development of communication skills in order to respect and facilitate choices made by the individual;
10. provide skill-building opportunities to enable individuals to participate in decision making relevant to leisure;
11. conduct assessment of individual capabilities and an analysis of the activity to determine level of participation (partial or full).

Examples of Recreation and Leisure Programs. These are programs in which individuals with deaf-blindness and other multiple profound handicaps can participate on varying levels:

Softball.

1. Full participation: the individual does the activity independently with necessary adaptations (noise in ball, ball on tee).
2. Partial participation:
   a. the individual runs from base to base with a peer partner;
   b. the individual in wheelchair is pushed by partner from base to base;
   c. given hand-over-hand assistance, the individual pitches the ball.

<u>Bicycle.</u>

1. Full participation: the individual rides independently with necessary adaptation (adult tricycle).
2. Partial participation: the individual rides on a tandem bicycle with another person.

<u>Watersports (Floating).</u>

1. Full participation: the individual floats in the pool with the only adaptation in doing so in the shallow end of the pool.
2. Partial participation: the individual wears a life preserver or arm floats or uses an inner tube.

<u>Additional examples where individuals can participate fully or partially.</u>

1. Community opportunities to derive multisensory experiences, such as amusement park rides, spectator sports, camping, fishing, hayrides, horseback riding, aerobics, roller skating, museums, and zoos with tactile (petting) sections.
2. Home/school opportunities, such as aerobics and swinging (for vestibular experiences), lotion application, fingerpainting, weaving, ceramics, and macrame.

Issues

Personnel

In order to bring about the programs described above, a variety of types of personnel with different training and experience will be required. These include professionals (e. g., therapeutic recreation specialists, recreation coaches, teachers, case managers) who will be needed for evaluating/assessing, planning, coordinating, implementing, and monitoring the newly mandated recreation and leisure programs. In addition, paraprofessionals and others including parents, volunteers, and peers will be needed to assist in these programs and in the hands-on participatory activities that may be required. These personnel may be employed in state, county, or community agencies as well as in schools, parks, and recreation departments, or in community and neighborhood projects.

In some cases, personnel may be currently available as existing staff who will be responsible for broadening their current responsibilities. To do so, they may be required to participate in further inservice training, depending on their expertise, in the following areas: recreation, leisure, alternative communication techniques, and the effects of the combined sensory impairments on individuals with deaf-blindness. In other instances and whenever possible, personnel who possess specialized training in the area of therapeutic recreation should be recruited. Many individuals in this field have only served in segregated settings, and now it is critical to utilize their expertise in the community.

Logistics Regarding Recreation and Leisure Programs

Appropriate management decisions should be considered in all logistical aspects. These aspects include availability.

1. Are the activities accessible? (These are concerns regarding transportation and architectural barriers.)
2. Are the activities available in home or local community?

Cost Factors

1. Which and how many staff members are needed?

2. What are the required fees, and are they valid, considering the preferences of the individual (e. g., horseback riding which is expensive and yet can be pleasurable to this population)?

Safety and Risk Factors

1. How is the consideration of the unique needs (such as health status) of the individual balanced with opportunities for pleasure which have some degree of risk involved (e. g., swimming and tubing)?
2. How can the service providers and parents balance the risk factors to maximally enhance the quality of life of the individual?

Recommendations

Implementation of Recreation and Leisure Programs

The group wholeheartedly recommended that wherever legislative responsibility exists for funding various types of programs, it should be mandated that recreation and leisure services, with characteristics such as those described above, be incorporated into the funded programs in order to ensure that each person with deaf-blindness and profound multiple handicaps has an appropriate recreation/leisure program within his own home community. For example, recreation/leisure programming should be included in the following:

1. Individual Education Plan (IEP),
2. Individual Transition Plan (ITP),
3. Individual Rehabilitation Plan (IRP),
4. Individual Habilitation Plan (IHP).

Communication

Appropriate communication is a necessary skill for all personnel, including volunteers, parents and significant others involved in the daily life of the person with deaf-blindness and profound multiple handicaps. The group strongly encourages the development and utilization of communication skills and alternative communication systems, modes, and strategies in the development and implementation of recreation and leisure programs.

Program Costs

Persons in this population need various support services. The individual with deaf-blindness and profound multiple handicaps has to maintain various levels of dependence upon various resources, including personnel, in order to survive and to grow. This necessary dependence requires an increased cost factor which is absolutely necessary in order to meet dependency needs.

Integration

Recreation and leisure programs should utilize existing community agencies and facilities which serve all persons. Appropriate personnel should help with any necessary preparation, awareness, and understanding of those with deaf-blindness and profound multiple handicaps prior to actual integration, if possible.

Continuity of Service

As these individuals come of age and leave the educational system, the following recommendations are made to ensure continuity of services:

1. The federal government should require states to designate a lead agency to be responsible for overall case management. This agency needs to maintain a quality assurance evaluation system for persons with deaf-blindness and other profound handicaps across life domains including residential, vocational, health, and recreation/leisure.
2. Parent representation should be included in all levels of decision making by the lead agency (from "board level" down).
3. The parent/guardian should be included in all planning and decision making concerning that individual's program from the very beginning.
4. The designated lead agency should have a recreation/leisure specialist to address individual recreation/leisure needs or coordinate with a specialist from a community recreation program to ensure appropriate recreation/leisure services.

SUMMARY

Summary, Conclusions, Recommendations, and Implications
of the Conference: Purpose and Format

Angela M. Covert

Purpose and Format of the Conference

The National Conference on the Transition of Profoundly/Multiply Handicapped Deaf-Blind Youth was a collaborative effort of Special Education Programs (U. S. Department of Education), Division of Maternal and Child Health Programs (U. S. Department of Health and Human Services), The Association for Persons with Severe Handicaps (TASH) Technical Assistance Project, and the Helen Keller National Center Technical Assistance Center (TAC). The overall purpose of the conference was to provide a multidisciplinary examination of the critical service needs of youth who are profoundly/multiply handicapped with deaf-blindness and who are old enough to be leaving the education system, and to recommend strategies for providing high quality comprehensive transition services for the youth and their families.

The objectives were as follows:

1. Examine the current transition service needs of youth with deaf-blindness and other profound handicaps and their families,
2. Describe the "state of the art" of available services,
3. Identify the service gaps and issues involved in providing high-quality transition services,
4. Recommend strategies for establishing optimal comprehensive transition services for youth who are profoundly/multiply handicapped with deaf-blindness and for the families of this population.

In examining comprehensive transition services, a major paper and two responses were presented in each of four areas:

1. residential services and options,
2. independent living and employment options,
3. recreation and leisure options,
4. health and psychosocial services

The presenters and respondents were asked to discuss the following:

1. the service needs of this population and their families;
2. the "state of the art" of available services for adolescents and adults with deaf-blindness and other profound handicaps;
3. the gaps in the services;
4. models and options to address the gaps in providing high-quality services for these youth and their families;
5. the needs of the systems providing services for this population, including interagency efforts;
6. the necessary support systems, including financing;
7. the implications for earlier education;
8. the role and involvement of parents and families.

The conference was designed as a "working conference" of approximately fifty invited participants with diverse backgrounds, including an interdisciplinary group of professionals in the field, policy makers, agency personnel and parents. Participants were drawn from education, rehabilitation services, health, and social service areas.

Each participant was preassigned to one of four groups which corresponded to the topic areas. The function of the groups was to consider the presentations and discussions, to identify the issues, and to formulate recommendations for program and policy. Each group spent a full day in a work session, and presented a group report the following morning. Summaries of the group reports are included in this book in their respective chapters.

Synthesis of Working Group Reports

Population

One issue that emerged in defining the population for the small working groups was whether the focus should be specifically on individuals who are deaf and blind, or whether the focus should encompass a broader population of individuals with profound multiple handicaps. The consensus was that because of the unique specialized needs of individuals with profound multiple sensory impairments, the working groups would focus specifically on persons who are profoundly/multiply handicapped with deaf-blindness. However, the groups agreed that the problems of accessibility to community-based services, the need to consider the individual in designing programs, and many of the issues and recommendations developed specifically for this population apply as well for all persons with profound handicaps.

The population was defined as a low-incidence population of individuals who are physiologically or functionally deaf-blind with additional profoundly handicapping conditions such as profound mental retardation and/or physical disabilities.

Additional characteristics of this population would include some or all of the following:

1. have developed only very limited communication skills;
2. lack independent mobility skills;
3. will need assistance in daily living skills, including feeding and toileting;
4. may exhibit severe behavioral disorders, including self-abusive and aggressive behavior:
   a. will require intensive, lifelong services such as medical care and physical, occupational, speech, and language therapies;
   b. will require lifelong assistance with skills and activities for integration in normal community environments.

The population includes those individuals described above who are of the age to be leaving, or have recently left, the mandated services of the public education system and are moving into the adult services systems.

Additionally, although not necessarily secondarily, the families of the target population were considered a significant part of the focus of this conference.

Philosophical Premises—Belief Statements

In considering what constitutes quality services for profoundly/multiply handicapped deaf-blind individuals, the working groups articulated a series of belief statements, creating the ethical framework, or _ethos_, of quality services. A synthesis of those belief statements follows:

1. All individuals, regardless of severity of handicapping conditions, have a fundamental right to individual dignity and the pursuit of happiness. They should be viewed as individuals, with individual rights, capabilities, and needs.
2. These individuals should have access to an array of adult services, with zero exclusion for eligibility in the adult services system, as in the education system.
3. Services provided for this population should aim toward full integration in the community and should enhance the quality of life of the individual, as well as his/her family, and include an array of options and choices to meet the individual's particular needs, desires, and interests.
4. Determination of any of the service options should be based on the individual's needs, abilities, and potential, and provide for continuing skill development, training, and education.
5. Services should be provided in settings that will foster interaction with others,

especially nonhandicapped individuals, as much as possible, and with and by individuals who are caring, respectful, and can overcome the communication barrier.

6. All individuals can benefit from and should have access to community-based services which provide for a small "homelike" residential arrangement as well as valued daily activities including vocational and employment options and recreation and leisure activities.

7. Profoundly multiply handicapped deaf-blind individuals, as other individuals, should have access to the benefits of our society, including comprehensive high-quality care of their physical and psychosocial needs.

8. In providing comprehensive transition services, residential options, work/employment options, recreation/leisure activities, and health and psychosocial services must be viewed as interdependent aspects of a person's life and cannot be considered as isolated services or foci.

9. Preparation for community-based independent living and the world of work should begin at the earliest age possible, and be designed to assist the individual and family to develop expectations, attitudes, skills, and experiences leading to integration in the community.

Program Approach – Characteristics

In defining high-quality programs/services for this population, which would reflect the ethos and values of the "belief statements," the following program approach and/or characteristics are delineated.

1. Programs/services for this population should recognize the unique communication and mobility problems of this population and be designed to meet the individualized needs of the client and his/her family, including options and choices for
    a. community-based living alternatives;
    b. employment/work options including supported work in business and industry;
    c. recreation and leisure activities on a daily basis;
    d. comprehensive health and psychosocial services that are individualized, are appropriate, promote wellness, and include support services for the families;
    e. full array of support services such as transportation, in-home respite care, and benefits.

2. Programs should occur in natural settings and foster continuing education, training, and skill development in communication, mobility, and self-care. Skill development should be future-oriented and directed toward lifelong use.

3. In recognition of the interdependence of the various components of comprehensive services, and to gain optimum benefit, an individualized case management system should be implemented to gain access to and coordinate the services across systems, develop assessment mechanisms, keep records, and share information, as appropriate, with other care providers.

4. All programs and program decisions should include a significant role for the parents and families. Not only is parent/family support essential for the success of community-based services, their expertise, knowledge, and understanding of the individual can enhance the potential for success. Programs and services must also consider and be responsive to the family's needs, interests, and preferences.

5. Personnel providing services for this population should be well trained and have skills in alternative communication systems to reduce the handicapped individual's isolation and improve his/her social integration.

6. Personnel should also be trained to diagnose, assess, and design programs that take into account the individual's auditory and visual ability, communications approach and skills, orientation and mobility training, self-preservation, and safety issues, and nonaversive behavior instruction.

7. Health issues must be considered in all living, work, and recreation environments,

and should be considered as part of the overall service plan.

8. Programs and services should have an evaluation component which reflects the values of the program and the quality-of-life issues for the individuals.

Issues and Recommendations

Developing and implementing high quality community-based transition services for this population presents many challenges and barriers. This section identifies a number of issues to be addressed and recommendations for improving transition services for individuals with deaf-blindness and other profound handicaps. While the list may seem extensive, it is not exhaustive.

Attitudes and Advocacy

Low public awareness, negative attitudes, and limited advocacy efforts constitute major barriers to providing high-quality, community-based services for individuals who are profoundly/multiply handicapped with deaf-blindness. Often the key to success of community-based programs depends on the attitudes, willingness, and support of local service agencies, vendors, businesses, and neighborhood residents. Yet for this population, there is low public awareness and understanding, low esteem, and low expectations, particularly regarding their potential to function in integrated community settings. Additionally, many professionals and service providers in the field hold limited expectations for this population, with somewhat negative attitudes toward their ability to be successful in community-based settings.

In order to improve community-based services, it will be essential to improve the advocacy efforts on behalf of this population and to improve the public awareness, understanding and expectations. Advocates for services to persons with profound multiple handicaps including deafness and blindness should form alliances with advocates for other low-incidence populations in order to increase their strength in advocating high-quality services. The advocacy efforts need to focus on obtaining new and improved services for this population, as well as gaining access to existing community-based services from which these individuals traditionally have been excluded.

Personnel - Training

There is a shortage of well-trained personnel including administrators, professionals, and paraprofessionals who can provide high-quality community-based services for this population. The shortage is evident in all areas such as residential, employment, recreation/leisure, and health/psychosocial, and at all levels, including state, county, and local agencies, programs, schools, parks, and health care agencies.

There is a lack of commitment from the higher education community, and a lack of incentive from the federal level to prepare personnel to provide services to low-incidence populations. Preservice training programs are needed to recruit, train, and retain new personnel, including leadership as well as service providers, for comprehensive, community-based services for this population. Also, there is need for inservice training for personnel who are providing services, but need to expand their range of competencies in areas such as the following:

1. developing specific competencies for working with individuals with deaf-blindness and other profound handicaps;
2. developing competencies for new roles such as that of job coach, recreation coach, therapeutic recreation specialist, community health care provider, community residence manager;
3. developing competencies for new settings, for example, staff who previously worked in segregated settings now may work in community-based, integrated settings.

151

Staff providing services for this population must be well trained, particularly in utilizing alternative communication systems and in understanding sensory deficits. New roles related to community-based services, that of job coach or recreation coach, need to be demonstrated with this population; the specific role competencies need to be identified, and the information disseminated.

Federal incentives are needed to support both preservice and inservice programs to encourage the recruitment, training, or retraining of qualified personnel for services to this population. Training programs should reflect the comprehensiveness of needed services and focus on a wide range of roles including those of leaders, teachers, counselors, health care providers, direct service providers, and new roles associated with community-based services.

Health care professionals and service providers need interdisciplinary training which equips them to provide a full range of health services. The training needs to include medical issues, psychosocial issues, and the specific needs of this population such as communication systems and adaptive aids and devices.

Program Accessibility

Programs and services for those who are profoundly/multiply handicapped with deaf-blindness should be designed to enable the individual to move as much as possible toward settings with nonhandicapped peers.

Individuals with profound multiple handicaps, as well as their families, need to be prepared for community-based living. Preparation, including education and skills training, should begin as early as possible, at least three years before the individual exits from the education system.

Many of the comprehensive community-based services are either not available to this population or are limited by financial issues, fiscal constraints of the family or logistical issues.

Community-based services not only must be available but also accessible. The lack of adequate and appropriate transportation often precludes access to some services. Another barrier often cited is the safety factor, with a need to strike a balance between the concern of the individual's safety against the risk of newer services.

Ongoing comprehensive services will be necessary to help these individuals to live in the community, but there has been a lack of commitment from agencies to provide the long-term funding for community-based services for the individual and for a system of supports for the family. Agencies need to recognize the importance and interdependence of comprehensive services, and provide program support for the community-based living, work, recreation/leisure, and health care. The programs should reflect the unique needs of this population, particularly with regard to communication systems.

Parent/Family Involvement

Providing services to this population must take into account parent/family needs, preferences, desires, and value systems. Parents and families need to be involved to enlist their support as well as their expertise, in all aspects and at every level, in providing comprehensive services for individuals with profoundly handicapping deafness and blindness. They need to be involved in decisions regarding the education and training of the individual with handicaps, as well as in the placement in community services. In order to strengthen the parent/family role, parents need to be provided with full information on options and choices open to them and to the handicapped child.

Parents/families often lack information on the range of services, including community-based services that are, or can be, available to them. Additionally, there is limited evidence to assure parents of the viability and benefits of community-based services for this profoundly handicapped population. Thus, lacking the necessary information on alternatives and the concomitant support system for the family, a concern for the care and safety of the handicapped individuals, and in consideration of the impact on other family members, parents frequently choose the more traditional, familiar services.

In addition to providing a support system for families, it is important to assist parents and families in increasing their knowledge, understanding, and acceptance of current trends in community-based transition services, to increase their expectations and aspirations for their handicapped family member, and to enlist their expertise and support in obtaining high-quality community-based services for their young adults.

There needs to be a nationwide strategy and commitment for parent/family involvement in transition services for this group. Models of comprehensive family support systems need to be developed and demonstrated to assist the parent/family involvement.

Policy- and Agency-Related Issues

Historically, there has been a reliance on institutions and segregated settings to provide services to individuals who are profoundly/multiply handicapped with deaf-blindness. With the increasing trend toward de-institutionalization, there has been an increase in the numbers and kinds of community-based services. However, because of the severity of the handicapping conditions and magnitude of necessary specialized services, this population generally has been excluded from those programs.

Public policy should reflect a commitment to providing comprehensive, high-quality, community-based transition services for all individuals, regardless of severity of handicap. The services should aim to foster independence and enhance the individual's quality of life. Financial commitments at the federal and state levels are essential as support to policy statements.

There is no overall mandate, with zero exclusions, to provide comprehensive adult services for individuals with handicaps. Adult service agencies are generally limited by laws and regulations in determining clients' eligibility for the services, including age limits, kinds of services supported, and length of time services can be provided. Generally, the eligibility requirements for community-based services have excluded populations requiring long-term comprehensive care.

Federal agencies and, in turn, state and local agencies need to recognize the newer, community-based services as viable options, eligible for support and funding. For example, the supported-work concept should be accepted by the Rehabilitation Services agencies as a viable "closure"; additionally, eligibility requirements of these agencies need to be expanded to include individuals with profound multiple handicaps of deaf-blindness who require comprehensive long-term care.

Because of the severity of the handicap, and the complexity of needed services, interagency efforts are essential, with case management provided by the lead agency. However, for the most part, there is no identified "lead agency" to provide leadership and coordinate services for this population. The interagency coordination is needed at all levels, including the federal level. The federal agencies such as Special Education Programs, Rehabilitation Services Administration, and Maternal and Child Health Programs should continue their collaborative efforts in support of services for these individuals. Further, their efforts should be expanded to include other relevant agencies such as the Administration for Developmental Disabilities, and National Institute for Mental Health. An interagency group should develop definitions for high quality comprehensive services, and guidelines to overcome agency barriers in providing the services.

Limited Knowledge Base

While many of the community-based services have been available to populations with other handicapping conditions, there is limited experience related to community-based services for those who are profoundly/multiply handicapped with deaf-blindness. The lack of knowledge presents a barrier in convincing parents/families, service providers, agency personnel, and policy makers of the viability of community-based services for these individuals and their families. There is need to define quality comprehensive services, identify models of quality or successful programs, delineate salient features and characteristics or best practices, and disseminate the information widely. Dissemination efforts should include information on high-quality community-based services as well as systems change models, including interagency-interdisciplinary models of service programs.

Additionally, research is needed to advance the knowledge base on understanding what kinds of services are viable and necessary for this population and their families. Issues such as client success in integrated settings, family involvement, and support services all need further study.

The federal government should provide fiscal support for further demonstration programs and for dissemination of information.

Conclusions and Implications

Transition and the Quality of Life

The basic premise of the conference was that while individuals with deaf-blindness and other profound handicaps may require lifelong care, they still can benefit from and should have full access to community-based services in the least restricted environment, and, with nonhandicapped peers, to the greatest possible extent. Thus, those services which aim to facilitate the transition of these individuals from education to adult living should have community integration as the goal, with quality of life as a major concern. The transition process should include opportunities to continue the learning and skill development that will enhance their living and independence; it should include options, alternatives and opportunities to make choices and decisions; and it should make available the information necessary for the individuals and their families to make informed choices.

Transition, one of the most overused words of recent years, has taken on many meanings. Perhaps the most common use of the word in reference to youth with handicapping conditions is to mean the "bridge between school and adult years," often viewed as "school to employment." While employment is a significant part, or outcome, of the transition process, it is just that: one part.

Transition for youth with deaf-blindness and other profound handicaps is a comprehensive process and should encompass a wide array of services. It is a process concerned with the total life of the individual, with facilitation of independent living to the greatest possible extent. The transition process must include planning and services for residential or living arrangements; employment options and ongoing building of skills; opportunities for recreation and leisure, as individuals or in groups; the health and social services to attend to the wellness of the individuals; and the necessary support services, such as transportation and respite care to make the other services accessible.

In the transition process, the primary focus should be on the individual, not on the services; programs should be developed to address the individual's needs rather than to fit the individual into the framework of available services. It is clear that the various aspects of transition services are interrelated and interdependent, just as the components of a person's life are interrelated and interdependent. The services need to be coordinated to form an integrated, comprehensive whole.

The Individual in Context of Family and Environment

The individual with deaf-blindness and other profound handicaps must be viewed in the context of his/her environment--the human environment as well as the physical environment. The individual is in constant interaction with his/her human environment, particularly with parents, family members, service providers, care givers, and others in the community. It is important to consider the environment when providing services, and provide the necessary support system to create a positive one.

Parents and families play a crucial role in the transition process, not only for the support and care which they provide, but also for their knowledge and expertise as their child moves into adult life. Parents often function as "case manager" for the child and should have a significant role in the planning and decision making at every level of the transition process.

In order to make informed decisions, parents must be provided with full and accurate information on the child's abilities and limitations, as well as the range of options and services available. The family's interests, needs, and desires must be considered in determining services and placements for the individual with handicaps. Further, a support system, including financial, social services, transportation, and respite care must be provided to enable families to maintain the young person in the community.

State of the Art of Services

In the past decade there has been great progress in providing high-quality, community-based services for persons with handicaps. However, these community-based services, for the most part, have not been available to persons with deaf-blindness and other profound handicaps. The state of the art of community-based services has not been advanced to the point of serving those persons with the most severe handicapping conditions. There may be a number of reasons why this is so. First, there has been a heavy reliance on traditional institutional settings for services to this population. Another reason may be that many service providers, as well as the general public, do not believe that this population can benefit from or be serviced in settings which are integrated in the community. Public policy and eligibility requirements for adult services do not provide a commitment to the long-term care and funding for community-based services for this population. Also, parents and families lacking information on the options and alternatives which could be available, and lacking evidence regarding the benefits and safety of community-based services, tend to rely on the traditional, well-known arrangements.

The presented papers and responses at the conference illustrated some exemplary community-based programs—programs which had been well developed, implemented, evaluated, and documented. While these programs represented state of the art in services, none were focused directly on individuals with deaf-blindness and other profound handicaps. It is clear that we have the technology for community-based services: The challenge is to build on the extant knowledge base and advance the state of the art to include this population.

Efforts need to be made to change public policy so that community-based services are accepted as viable options, with full support, for individuals who need comprehensive lifelong care. Providing comprehensive transition services requires a sharing of responsibility and resources between and among agencies at all levels—federal, state, and local—and among parents and families, local service providers, and community residents. Eligibility requirements for service may need to be altered, and agency boundaries may need to be crossed to provide coordinated services and support. Further, federal agencies should require states to identify a "lead agency" to be responsible for coordinating services among and between agencies, to provide the leadership in negotiating between agencies, and to overcome turf barriers in providing coordinated, comprehensive services.

Staff and Training

Staff providing services to this population need to be well trained for a range of roles including those of teachers, counselors, and administrators, as well as for new roles such as job coach and community residence managers. Staff need to understand the effects of profoundly handicapping conditions, have competency in alternative communication systems, and knowledge of the most advanced state of the art of community-based service.

In addition to new skills and competencies, providing services in community-based settings places new demands and expectations on staff who have been working in the more traditional institutional settings. For some, it may mean functioning in new ways and, in a sense, renegotiating their roles. In working as part of multidisciplinary teams, it may mean overcoming turf barriers and collaborating with other agencies, or it may mean working in collaboration with parents and family members as full partners.

In order to ensure quality transition services for youth with deaf-blindness and other profound handicaps, it is necessary to encourage new training programs such as preservice training programs to recruit new staff at all levels to the field, and inservice training programs for those service providers who need, or want, to extend their range of competencies. It is essential that the federal government provide incentives for the higher education community to prepare staff to work with low-incidence populations.

Dissemination and Advocacy

With a limited base of knowledge, we need to identify and document the best of the technology, the art and science of serving those with deaf-blindness and other profound handicaps. There is need to identify or develop some exemplary models, identify the salient or critical features, and disseminate information widely for the purposes of illustrating what can be done, as well as how this population can benefit from these services.

Advocacy efforts on behalf of this low-incidence population need to be strengthened in order to obtain new or improved services. One means of accomplishing this would be to build coalitions with other advocacy groups. While recognizing the specialized needs of those individuals with deaf-blindness and the need to maintain specialized services, advocacy groups can work together to try to eliminate sharp barriers between those with deaf-blindness and other populations. With the increased strength of their combined efforts, advocacy groups can work toward improving services for all youth and adults with profound multiple handicaps, with a goal of continuing the guarantee of rights to services after reaching age 22 and throughout the adult years.

Concluding Statement

Transition, a word with many meanings, is used in this book, and was used in the conference which served as the basis for this book, to refer to the passage from school-age years to adult living. The population of concern are those individuals with deaf-blindness and other profound handicaps.

An underlying theme of the conference and a commitment of the participants is that transition is an ongoing process which should lead to community integration for the individual, regardless of severity of handicapping condition. It is a process concerned with the total life of the individual, with programs and services determined on the basis of the individual's abilities as well as disabilities, the individual's strengths as well as needs. It is a process that views the individual in the context of his/her environment--human and physical--and aims to improve the individual's quality of life in that environment. It is an outcome-oriented process that includes an array of services leading to options and choices in community-based living arrangements, work opportunities, recreation and leisure activities, and the health and psychosocial services, all of which are interrelated and interdependent just as the aspects of a person's life are interrelated and interdependent. It is a process that delivers services to achieve those outcomes in a comprehensive, coordinated manner. And, it also is also a process that considers the individuals' parents, families, and community and provides a support system for them as well.

The conference and this book have focused on the specialized needs of persons with profound multiple handicaps of deaf-blindness. However, the results of the conference indicate that many of the problems and issues involved in accessibility to high-quality programs, the comprehensiveness of needed services for the individuals as well as their families, and the recommendations for improving transition services that lead to the individual's integration in the community apply as well to all individuals with profound handicaps.

Advancing the state of the art of community-based services to include those individuals with deaf-blindness and other profound handicaps presents new demands and challenges for all of us who are the policy makers, the professionals and service providers, the parents and families, and the community. It requires us to think and work in new ways, to cross the boundaries of classrooms and agencies, to interact in new ways with parents, families, and personnel in other systems, and even to redefine our roles in providing services to individuals with profound handicaps. In a sense, it is a time of transition for us as well.

CONFERENCE PARTICIPANTS

Mr. Martin A. Adler
Director
Helen Keller National Center
111 Middle Neck Road
Sands Point, NY   11050

Mr. Stephen Barrett
Assistant Project Director
Helen Keller National Center
Technical Assistance Center
1111 W. Mockingbird Lane
Suite 1330
Dallas, TX   75247

Dr. Thomas Behrens
Director
Division of Innovation
   and Development
Special Education Programs
400 Maryland Avenue
Washington, DC   20202

Dr. Hank Bersani
Project Coordinator
Research and Training Center
   on Community Integration
123 College Place
Syracuse, NY   13244-4130

Dr. Joann Boughman
Division of Human Genetics
University of Maryland
   at Baltimore
655 W. Baltimore Street
Baltimore, MD   21201

Mr. Richard Bunner
Supervisor
Vision Conservation Program
Ohio Department of Health
Maternal Child Health
246 North High Street
Columbus, OH   43266-0588

Ms. Terry Carr
Program Associate
Helen Keller National Center
Technical Assistance Center
111 Middle Neck Road
Sands Point, NY   11050

Ms. Stephanie Campo
Program Director
Chief Executive Officer
Special Children's Village, Inc.
12009 Florida Boulevard
Baton Rouge, LA   79815

Ms. Rose Ceisla
Deaf-Blind Multihandicapped
   Consultant
New Hampshire Education Services
   for Sensory Impaired
17 South Fruit Street
Concord, NH   03301

Mr. Michael T. Collins
Educational Supervisor
Perkins School for the Blind
175 N. Beacon Street
Watertown, MA   02172

Dr. Angela Covert
Project Director
Helen Keller National Center
Technical Assistance center
111 Middle Neck Road
Sands Point, NY   11050

Dr. John Datillo
Assistant Professor
5203 Henderson
Recreation and Parks Dept.
Pennsylvania State University
State College, Pennsylvania   16802

Ms. Anne Devereux
Parent Representative
IL Advisory Board for Services
   for Deaf-Blind Individuals
735 Wesley
Oak Park, IL   60304

Ms. Mary Dickson
Director of Rehab. Services
Oregon Commission for the Blind
535 SE 12th Avenue
Portland, OR   97214

Dr. Terrance Dolan
Medical Director
Coordinator of Clinical Services
Waisman Center
  on Mental Retardation
  and Human Development
1500 Highland Avenue
University of Wisconsin-Madison
Madison, WI 53705

Mr. David Esquith
Office on Governmental Affairs
National Association for
  Retarded Citizens
1522 K Street NW, Suite 56
Washington, DC 20005

Dr. Patricia Fleming
Consultant
Helen Keller National Center
Technical Assistance Center
111 Middle Neck Road
Sands Point, NY 11050

Dr. Sharon Freagon
Associate Professor
Northern Illinois University
LDSE, Graham Hall, NIU
DeKalb, IL 60115

Dr. H. D. Bud Fredericks
Director
TASH Technical Assistance
  Central Office
345 N. Monmouth Avenue
Monmouth, OR 97361

Mr. Charles Freeman
Project Officer
Special Education Programs
330 C Street SW
Switzer Building, Room 4607
Washington, DC 20202

Ms. Lillian Garcia
President
Florida Association for
  the Deaf-Blind and
  Multiply Handicapped
1741 Jefferson Road
Jacksonville, FL 32216

Dr. Lori Goetz
Associate Professor
Department of Special Education
San Francisco State University
612 Font Boulevard
San Francisco, CA 94132

Mr. David Goode
University Affiliated Facility
Mental Retardation Institute
New York Medical Center
Valhalla, NY 10595

Ms. Dorothy Hallett
Dept. of Health, Family-Health
  Services Division
Community Services for
  D. D. Branch
Community Program Section
3627 Kilauea Avenue
Room 106
Honolulu, HI 96816

Dr. Sharon Hostler
Attending Physician
Children Rehabilitation Center
2270 Ivy Road
Charlottesville, VA 22901

Dr. William E. Jones
Executive Director
American Association of
  Univ. Affiliated Programs
8605 Cameron Street
Suite 406
Silver Spring, MD 20910

Dr. Virginia Lapham
Georgetown University
Child Development Center
3800 Reservoir Road, NW
Washington, DC 20007

Mr. Kevin Lessard, Director
Perkins School for the Blind
175 North Beacon Street
Watertown, MA 02172

Mr. Norman McCallum
1236 North June
Hollywood, CA 90038

Ms. Patricia J. McCallum
Executive Director
Chairperson
Statewide Transition Task Force
Deaf-Blind Multihandicapped
    Association of Texas
815 High School Drive
Seagoville, TX 75159

Dr. Merle McPherson
Acting Director
Division of Maternal and
    Child Health
5600 Fishers Lane-Room 6-05
Rockville, MD 20857

Mrs. Caye Nelson
Director
Ramsey County Extension
    Services (4-H)
2020 White Bear Avenue
St. Paul, MN 55109

Ms. Nancy Norman, Director
Iowa Commission for the Blind
524 Fourth Street
Des Moines, IA 50309

Ms. Mary O'Donnell, President
New Jersey Association
    for the Deaf-Blind
2 Whitney Terrace
Verona, NJ 07044

Ms. Nancy O'Donnell
Project Coordinator
Helen Keller National Center
Technical Assistance Center
111 Middle Neck Road
Sands Point, NY 11050

Ms. Jane Polcaro
Parent/Advocate
Apparent Concern Inc.
417 Turtleback Road
Marston Mills, MA 02648

Ms. Beth Quarles
Deaf-Blind Specialist
Texas Rehab Commission
118 E. Riverside Drive
Austin, TX 78704

Ms. Shirley Rees
Community Relations Specialist
Bureau of Community Services
429 - O Street, NW
Washington, DC 20202

Dr. Lyle Romer
Coordinator of Neighborhood
    Living Project
1700 E. Cherry Street
Seattle, WA 98122

Ms. Barbara Ryan
Parent Specialist, ICSM
Special Education Resource
    Network
5203 El Cerrito Drive #255
Riverside, CA 92507

Dr. Rosanne Silberman
Associate Professor, Coordinator
Programs for Severely/Multiply
    Handicapped and Visually Handicapped
Hunter College - CUNY
695 Park Avenue
Box 1487
New York, NY 10021

Mr. Frank Simpson
National Consultant on Employment
American Federation for the Blind
15 West 16th Street
New York, NY 10011

Mr. George Singer
Research Scientist
oregon Research Institute
1899 Willamette Street
Eugene, OR 97401-4015

Ms. Anne Smith
Consultant
Helen Keller National Center
Technical Assistance Center
111 Middle Neck Road
Sands Point, NY 11050

Dr. R. Paul Thompson
Chief, Special Needs Section
Special Education Programs
400 Maryland Avenue, SW
Switzer Building - Room 4615
Washington, D.C. 20202

Ms. Nancy Trenbeth
Teacher Consultant for
  PMH/DB Youth
Shoreline School District
117 NW 188th
Seattle, WA 98177

Ms. Deirdre R. Trent
Department of Human Services
Mental Retardation
  D.D. Administration
429 - O Street
Washington, DC 20001

Mr. Philip Wade
Principal
Helen Keller School
Alabama Institute for
  the Deaf-Blind
P.O. Box 698
Talladega, AL 35160

Mrs. R. Carol Wallenstein
8 Kent Street
Concord, NH 03301

Dr. Paul Wehman
Rehabilitation Research
  and Training Center
Virginia Commonwealth University
Box 2011
Richmond, VA 23284-0001

PLANNING COMMITTEE

Dr. H. D. Bud Fredericks, Co-Chair
Director
TASH TA Central Office

Mr. Stephen Barrett
Assistant Project Director
HKNC Technical Assistance Center

Dr. Thomas Behrens
Director
Division of Information
  and Development
Special Education Programs

Dr. Joann Boughman
Division of Human Genetics
University of Maryland

Mr. Aaron Favors
Division of Maternal and
  Child Health

Mr. Charles W. Freeman
Project Officer
Special Needs Section
Special Education Programs

Mr. Dick Galloway
Executive Director
National Association of State
  Directors of Special Education

Dr. Lori Goetz
Department of Special Education
San Francisco State University

Dr. Angela M. Covert, Co-Chair
Project Director
HKNC Technical Assistance Center

Dr. William Grimm
Ohio Department of Health
Maternal and Child Health

Dr. Sharon Hostler
Attending Physician
Children's Rehabilitation Center

Mr. Bob Jones
Program Specialist
R.S.A.
Dept. of Education

Dr. Virginia Lapham
Child Development Center
Georgetown University

Dr. Merle McPherson
Acting Director
Division of Maternal and
  Child Health

Dr. R. Paul Thompson
Chief, Special Needs Section
Special Education Programs

Mrs. Carol Wallenstein
Parent